AUTISM
ALL-STARS

by the same author

Set for Success
Activities for Teaching Emotional, Social and Organisational Skills
Josie Santomauro and Margaret-Anne Carter
Foreword by Damian Santomauro
ISBN 978 1 84905 058 6

of related interest

The Complete Guide to Asperger's Syndrome
Tony Attwood
ISBN 978 1 84310 495 7 hardback
ISBN 978 1 84310 669 2 paperback

Voices from the Spectrum
Parents, Grandparents, Siblings, People with Autism,
and Professionals Share Their Wisdom
Edited by Cindy N. Ariel and Robert A. Naseef
ISBN 978 1 84310 786 6

The Passionate Mind
How People with Autism Learn
Wendy Lawson
Foreword by Rita Jordan
ISBN 978 1 84905 121 7

Finding a Different Kind of Normal
Misadventures with Asperger Syndrome
Jeanette Purkis
Foreword by Donna Williams
ISBN 978 1 84310 416 2

An Exact Mind
An Artist With Asperger Syndrome
Peter Myers, Simon Baron-Cohen and Sally Wheelwright
ISBN 978 1 84310 032 4

The Feeling's Unmutual
Growing Up With Asperger Syndrome (Undiagnosed)
Will Hadcroft
ISBN 978 1 84310 264 9

AUTISM ALL-STARS

HOW WE USE OUR AUTISM AND ASPERGER TRAITS TO SHINE IN LIFE

EDITED BY JOSIE SANTOMAURO

FOREWORD BY TONY ATTWOOD

Jessica Kingsley *Publishers*
London and Philadelphia

First published in 2012
by Jessica Kingsley Publishers
116 Pentonville Road
London N1 9JB, UK
and
400 Market Street, Suite 400
Philadelphia, PA 19106, USA

www.jkp.com

Library of Congress Cataloging in Publication Data
Autism all-stars : how we use our autism and Asperger traits to shine in life / edited by Josie Santomauro ; foreword by Tony Attwood.
   p. cm.
 ISBN 978-1-84310-188-8 (alk. paper)
 1. Asperger's syndrome. I. Santomauro, J. (Josie)
 RC553.A88A487 2012
 616.85'8832--dc23
                                     2011030596

British Library Cataloguing in Publication Data
A CIP catalogue record for this book is available from the British Library

ISBN 978 1 84310 188 8
eISBN 978 0 85700 600 4

Printed and bound in Great Britain

This book is dedicated to its contributors:

Rob, Donna, Jeanette, Peter, Wendy, Stephen, Deborah, Will, Leith, Mark, Jessica, Stan, Iain, Temple, Damian, Malcolm, Colin, Sondra and Roger.

I thank them for their courage and honesty in sharing these stories, and in accentuating in particular the positives and successes that their particular diagnosis has brought into their lives.

I sincerely thank my publisher, Jessica Kingsley, and her dedicated and very professional staff for believing in this project through its ups and downs over the ten years. We made it!

CONTENTS

FOREWORD

Tony Attwood

Someone who has autism has a brain that is wired differently, which can lead to amazing talents and achievements. This book describes how 19 individuals with autism have approached their being different positively and constructively, and benefited from the gifts of autism.

In the typical brain, there is a preference for noticing and analyzing social information – for example, to prioritize the information conveyed in someone's facial expression rather than the shape of his ears. In autism, the brain notices, and finds interesting and informative, other aspects of experience. My simple definition of autism is that the person has found something more interesting in life than socializing.

I am an amateur gardener and enjoy using this metaphor for brain development: it is like the creation of a new garden where the plants represent structures within the brain. The typical child's garden is dominated by a quickly growing and flourishing tree, which creates a canopy of leaves that absorbs sunlight and enhances the growth of the tree, and a deep root structure that makes the tree resilient by absorbing the nutrients and moisture in the soil. The umbrella canopy of leaves shades and thus inhibits the growth of other plants in the garden. These plants also have less access to nutrients and moisture, which further inhibits their development. This dominant tree represents the social structures within the brain of a typical child or adult who devotes a great deal of brain activity and time to socializing. In Asperger's syndrome, the same potential "tree" only grows to become a bush; in severe autism, a flower. However, in these cases, other plants are not inhibited, and can thus take advantage of the opportunity to flourish.

From my clinical experience, when a person has autism there are several neurological "plants" that become larger than they would in a typical neurological "garden". The most common is the development of a natural expertise in engineering and information technology. These abilities are based on advanced logic and visual reasoning rather than interpersonal skills. Other "plants" that flourish include mathematical and musical abilities; the ability to draw with photographic realism; and a talent in conveying emotions and the self through art forms such as creative writing and dance, rather than through conversation.

It is inevitable that the child who has autism will at some stage recognize that he or she is different from other children. A constructive response to this realization is to observe people in order to analyze their behaviour and motives, or to become an expert mimic in order to be accepted and included. This can lead to a successful career as a psychologist or an actor.

It is important for families and clinicians to acknowledge the personality of the person who has autism, since this is fundamental to his or her choice of career. That person may show great concern for the well-being of others, and a sense of social justice that leads to a valued and rewarding career in the caring and teaching professions. People who have autism can also be very determined and tenacious, and have great courage, despite the adversity of suffering criticism and rejection by peers. The contributors to this book are genuine and representative *Autism All-Stars* who have all made constructive use of abilities that have been enhanced by autism. Their stories will encourage and inspire those who have autism, and their families and teachers.

INTRODUCTION

Josie Santomauro

As with all my written works, this book took me on a journey. This journey began nearly ten years ago when I travelled to London. While jetlagged, I ventured into the offices of Jessica Kingsley Publishers, and as an unknown author of special needs resources I presented the idea of this book to Jessica Kingsley herself. That is where this journey was kick-started, a contract drawn up, and the idea began to roll. Albeit a very long roll, but by the end I have gathered the most amazing contributors. My contributors and I made similar journeys; as the manuscript developed over the years, so did their stories.

As a published fiction author, I know that before a book is created the idea is first conceived. I also know that different creators have varied ways of conceiving these ideas. There was a time during the early years of my son Damian's diagnosis where I felt disillusioned and depressed from the countless negative and sad stories that came from some of the autism spectrum disorders (ASD) community. Not only were these stories from persons with ASD, but also their carers and advocates. As a mother of a newly diagnosed child, I wanted to hear success stories, I needed to be enlightened, and I craved positivity. *Where were all the good news stories?* But just as we watch the daily news and switch off the television feeling a little down about the world's torments, the news of the ASD world left me feeling just as down, focusing on the daily torments, burdens and failures of our children, adults and the systems. Education facilities and specialists focused on the negative characteristics. But amongst these lists of characteristics were one or two positive gems; namely, expertise in their field of obsession. This is where my light bulb turned on, and a question formulated in my mind.

That question being, "What is it about ASD that has had a positive and successful influence and impact in their lives?" I wanted the world to see ASD in a new light, to share stories that are successful, uplifting and challenging at the same time. I was determined to scour the earth for these stories and am honoured to present you with these stories from persons with ASD of varying nationalities, diagnoses, backgrounds and ages.

I have learnt so much from my contributors' stories. They have enlightened and inspired me with not only their successful tales but also their ongoing gifts to the world.

Persons with ASD provide and have always provided us with brilliant theatrical productions, latest inventions, ahead-of-the-times computer software, classic novels, scientific research, explorations, renaissance art, philosophy, politics, classical music, even Nobel prizes.

ASD communities – can we deliver successful, positive good news stories? As Barack Obama said… Yes we can!

Welcome to the wonderful world of ASD.

PART 1

EDUCATION

The following three contributions reminisce and share their past and current schooling years where they learnt many life lessons.

Some common school challenges for a person with ASD are the bullying, behavioural problems, and a lack of understanding social cues. Consequently a school day can be emotionally exhausting for a person on the spectrum.

The earlier the diagnosis and intervention, the easier school life may become. Alternatively there are other options, including home schooling and/or part-time schooling at a school specifically for children with ASD.

Finding the right pieces to the puzzle can be the key to successful schooling.

- *Jessica Peers* shares her days as a "Vampire Aspie" and how she doodled her way through college/university to combat her attempts to fit in and socialise.

- *Stan Hood* proves that you're never too old to study and takes pride in the fact that in his early sixties he is finally attending university.

- *Iain Payne* defines how during his university studies he finally received a diagnosis of Asperger syndrome; and how it changed his life in a positive way.

CHAPTER 1

AN EDUCATION IN DOODLING

Jessica Peers

Behind the band names and cartoon animals that danced across my folder, I carefully altered the nose of my latest creation. Her hair was great: long, flowing waves, a disco star strewn here and there, her eyes with those "look at me" lashes and inky glare. Even the beauty spot above the mouth was perfect, but somehow the nose didn't quite fit.

"Wow! That really does look like Madonna!" said Vicky in a loud whisper.

"Think so? I really don't think I've done the nose very well."

The image scrawled with biro did not match the image in my head. Worse still: my pen was leaking. Looking down on my hands, they were zebra-striped with black ink.

"Hey!" nudged Pammie. "We're supposed to be listening to Grant's lecture on T.S. Eliot, not drawing pop stars."

Slightly embarrassed, I flipped to a clean page and started work on a Kate Moss that would never match up to the David Bowie in *Labyrinth* I doodled during Theory of Criticism. In truth, I was far more interested in doodling than I was in T.S. Eliot. I had found *The Waste Land* both pretentious and unintelligible.

Before forcedly reading the book and then using it as a coffee-coaster, my only knowledge of Mr Eliot had been through Andrew Lloyd Webber's *Cats*, which I had enjoyed only because it, predictably, featured cats.

Doodling was my escape. Sometimes trying to fit in, even with the Goths and misfits I hung around with, was hard. Some people dressed bohemian, yet inside were rather conservative. Although I had been taught to be conservative and keep my head down whilst in care, I yearned to be rebellious. However, spray-painting "HELL HERE" across the newly painted walls of my flat only caused an irremovable stain and my collage of rock idols and screen dreams could only hide it in earnest. The walls of my bedroom had been painted a melancholic purple, and the room was truly melancholic due to there being one broken heater and the draughty rush of traffic from the main road outside. From overhead the strains of my neighbour's beloved Bryan Adams collection could be heard. I never complained as the sounds of other people's lives could be more comforting than had I moved to a ghost town.

The flat had not been of my choosing and I had protested greatly at moving out of care. On moving I tried to convince the support workers that the flat was haunted by poltergeists.

To enforce this factor, I accidentally set off the fire alarm after trying to cook an egg in the microwave. Little did I know that smoke would soon billow from the clunky piece of redundant 1980s technology and set off what sounded like a disco in Afghanistan. After the "fire" incident, I begged to be returned to care, yet to no avail.

I was supposed to be *independent.* That word was a curse. The F-word, the C-word and even the worst of expletives paled into comparison. I had no choice but to fit in, yet retain an aura of "difference" so as not to appear dull, or worse still, invisible.

My three main friends, Vicky, Pammie and Ruth, were all outgoing characters. Vicky was the smart one with sexy tattoos, a loud Geordie accent and great figure: the attractive one, and the leader. Pammie was the kooky one with her Jimi Hendrix hair and love of velvet. When I found out that her father was a vicar, I was surprised. Ruth was the youngest, the flirty one, and the dizzy six-foot tall blonde.

In contrast, I was the quiet one, the shy and reliable one, the nice one whose hair was always clean and the one who couldn't speak to a man without staring over his shoulder. I dared not open my mouth too often in case I put my platform-booted size-5 feet in it. Aspie people are notorious for saying odd things and I was not going to be one of them. I remember the story of a care-home trip when a boy called Jake loudly passed wind and everyone complained of the smell. Another Aspie boy named Pete turned around and grinned "I'm enjoying the smell!" much to the amusement of the staff. Worse still, I remembered when an Aspie boy had chatted me up by saying I looked "good for an older woman" – I was a mere six months his senior. I was not going to make these "Aspie" mistakes. No, I thought, I'll stay quiet, mysterious and creative.

My real personality revealed itself only in the stars, faces, animals, flowers and the tumbledown houses that I drew when I was supposed to be listening to the lecturer rant about a long-dead conservative poet I had not bothered to read. Had the lecture been on Mary Shelley, Lord Byron or Dostoevsky, I might have taken more interest, but my mind found it hard to focus. I needed to feel passion for the subject in order to listen. Sometimes I could hear the words, but not the meaning, rather like watching a film and forgetting the plot. It sounded as if the lecturer was reciting an Ikea manual, or a train timetable, or, worse still, a bank statement. I was not unintelligent, but my mind would sometimes become a blank sheet of paper, just *waiting* to be filled up with doodles. Doodling had an advantage: it made me look, from a distance, as if I was writing notes, when really I was drawing a dagger flying into a tattooed heart or an eye weeping diamond tears. They were also a great distraction from boredom.

After a lecture, we would go to the student bar to cool off and discuss the lecture. Before meeting my friends, I had not liked to drink alcohol, preferring just to go home and read, but I would sit there, enjoying a cold pint of cider, trying to look intelligent. I started to like cider as it tasted like apple pop and helped me open up. Besides, it was the *official drink* of Sunderland Goths. With my inky-black short bob, and red lipstick, I was part vampire, part Snow White. Most of the people our gang got on with were Goths.

The Goths were intelligent, morbidly witty and generally eccentric: rather like Aspies in their outsider status, so I would drink at the Union bar with the Goths, put The Smashing Pumpkins on the jukebox and read people's tarot with my own pack of cards. One thing I had learned was that the tarot client *always* wanted to know about their love life.

Love was Vicky's favorite subject, alongside sex and men in general. Unbeknown to most, at 19, I had not yet had a steady boyfriend, so I fabricated an imaginary "Darren" and "Colin", along with their bad dress sense and ugly shoes. I was still uncomfortable around men, but put my acting skills into gear.

"Darren's coming over with his terrible music collection," I would sigh, smiling. "I might write to Colin, who lives in

London. He's starting his own business." Nobody really seemed interested.

I had never been in love, but it seemed exciting. On my bedroom wall were posters of beautiful Argentine footballers and handsome singers in bands. I imagined that Vicky could have flirted with any of them and not felt nervous. Vicky made love seem so racy, so dangerous and exciting. I watched her for tips on flirting. Whenever we went clubbing, she would always know the right way to chat up a man. Noticing how she smiled and made jokes, I picked this up. I'd chatted to a couple of men and had started to open up to them: sometimes I even smiled. I had read that pouting and appearing too moody could put other people off. Sometimes I couldn't *help* but pout: I always pouted when I was trying to concentrate or get something right.

"Know something, Jessy?" giggled Vicky over a Jack Daniels and coke, as she gracefully stubbed out her cigarette.

"What?" I raised my head from my latest doodle masterpiece.

"Have you ever noticed that T.S. Eliot is an anagram of 'toilets'?" The whole bar guffawed in unison. A few hours later we were enjoying Chaucer. I loved Chaucer as my mother had given me *The Canterbury Tales* to read and, once I had translated it into modern English, I had enjoyed most of it. For a presentation once, I had dressed up as my favourite character, The Wife of Bath, complete with rosy-red *sanguine* cheeks. For authenticity, I had pencilled a gap between my teeth for The Wife's *Mark of Venus* and padded myself up to her legendary proportions.

In character, I felt safe. I was somebody else. I was acting. Unrecognisable beneath the towel masquerading as a medieval headdress and the busty padding, I let her persona take me over. I was no longer shy; I was an actress playing a role. Even in my Goth role I could hide myself by dyeing my naturally indecisive brown-blonde-ginger hair black and wearing more make-up than Boy George on one of his better days. I could even find extravagantly fluffy black coats to match the gang with. We all competed to see who could find the most heinous coat on our regular trawls around the charity shops – and once mine nearly beat Vicky's! The coat was like a little black shell I could hide in.

At the Union bar and in lectures, I played another role. I appeared as normal in behaviour as a vampire Aspie could be.

Inside, the obsessions were just fighting to get out, to pop from my lips like a broken bubble. If there was no soap in the toilets, I would become agitated, but hide it. I wanted to talk on and on about bands I liked, but I knew they were never "Goth" enough. I was playing a role. Carefully, I held the obsessions back. I was a great actress, hiding all my little oddities from my friends…or so I *thought*.

"Is that a panther?" asked Ruth. "Or is it a leopard?"

"Don't know," I replied, "I've not shaded it in yet."

"You're *always* drawing, Jessy," noticed Pammie.

"Draw *me*!" said Vicky.

Carefully, I studied her face. Scanning her Celtic green eyes and red hair, I imagined how to shade them in on paper.

"That's a real good likeness!" said Vicky, glancing down at the inky image.

"Just hope I got your nose right!" I laughed.

As I cheekily drew her a pair of fangs, I thought to myself: *maybe Aspies aren't that different from vampires after all?* Vampires were outsiders, viewed with suspicion over odd behaviours, sometimes concealed their identities as vampires from the mortal world. I concealed my Aspie identity from the neurotypical world.

Looking at the old folders and jotters I have kept from my student days, I see the people I knew, the people I still know, the people I wanted to be, all mingling amongst the towering spires and gardens of skulls. I still doodle, sometimes to entertain people and leave them a little souvenir. My current boyfriend noticed he was perpetually drawn without a nose.

"Is that just a fixation of yours?" he asked.

"No, Big Fella. It's just that your nose isn't that noticeable."

Secretly, I laughed, then planned my next portrait.

Since writing this, I have moved on from the "Big Fella" without a nose and sometimes, in passing, see my old university friends. All three are happily married. Due to my bad luck with men, I passed my degree with a First, a secret swottiness that I never told my friends. I am all too aware that it can be difficult for Aspies to form relationships. All too aware that I may appear a "Judas" for writing this, I admit that I could never have a relationship with an Aspie man. If I were having a fat day, he would probably agree that I was fat, or if my hair had been cut badly he would say so. My confidence would be reaching for the gin bottle and a sneaky cigarette! However, Aspie relationships *can* exist – they just take more time and patience than most. There have been Aspie marriages, even full Aspie families. As with all relationships, they depend on the two people involved, Asperger or not.

Jessica, diagnosed with Asperger syndrome at age 12, spent most of her education in a residential school for young people with autism. She has just completed her PhD in Asperger and Life Narratives, is a voluntary researcher at the Autism Research Unit (University of Sunderland) and writes in her spare time.

CHAPTER 2

THE UGLY DUCKLING

Stan Hood

In 1963, at the age of 18 and in my last year of schooling, I turned down my mother's offer to send me to university, even though she and I believed that I could handle it. My academic record thus far, although patchy, did show that at my best, I was indeed the best, as far as marks in exams went. On the other hand, when I had no interest in a subject at school, I came last in the exams. I had no idea that, over 40 years later, my old school reports, showing such wild swings between being first or last with not so many average marks in the middle, would be one small piece of evidence for my formal diagnosis of Asperger syndrome (AS).

Learning new things had always been a joy to me, especially in the science or engineering realms. I had enjoyed studying at school, in selected subjects. However, if at any time the school had been light on teaching what I considered "good" subjects, there was always the city library with all those science books. I read voraciously.

In all my school years, AS was unknown. But I did understand more and more as my schooling progressed that I had a whole bunch of seemingly unconnected "natural" traits, which decades later I found were typical of those with AS. I had come to realize of my own volition that I had an outlook on life that was different to my schoolmates. I had a nervous disposition. I was very kind-hearted. I was introverted. My speech was so bad that I had to have special coaching (this was so successful that around the age of 12 or 13, I was topping the class in speaking and reading exercises). I did not like team sports. My slightly poor sense of balance held me back in school gymnastics periods (I was not to realize until my thirties that I also ran with a slightly strange gait, another of those oddball AS traits). I preferred books to friends. One friend was as much as I ever wanted.

During my school years I think the kids might have realized that I was a bit different to them, both in outlook and physical abilities. They must have noticed too that I always seemed to have at least one friend. Certainly I acquired a reputation for helping some of the kids with understanding their lessons. They gave me the nickname of "professor", which I accepted with good grace. Possibly, unlike some people with AS (or Aspies, as we have come to be known), I did not suffer too much from schoolyard bullies because I was seen to be positively interacting with some of the neurotypical kids in those few ways.

But in my older school years it became harder to talk myself out of attempted bullying situations. Even so, there was only one time at secondary school when I was forced to get physical with a boy who refused to listen to my many polite requests over a six-month period to stop bad-mouthing and pushing me. On the day I belted him one, with meaning, I became probably the only pupil in the history of the school to bring my school's formal morning assembly to an unexpected sudden halt.

Then I walked out of school, highly distressed at being forced into doing something like that out of frustration. When I reached home I threw all my schoolbooks outside and vowed I would never return to school again. Thankfully I had some wonderful and understanding teachers who combined forces with my parents and finally persuaded me to go back to school. I did, for two more years, and continued to achieve my remarkably good and remarkably bad results.

After that event, my English teacher, who knew me as a quiet, shy boy, derived great amusement from calling me a pugilist over the incident, a boxer or a person who fights with their fists. That certainly gained peals of laughter from the rest of the class because everybody knew very well just how much I was not one of those. By then I was able to share good-naturedly in the laughter.

Why people deliberately want to annoy quiet, gentle people is beyond me. Intellectually I now understand it, but I don't myself do that sort of asserting power or authority over others. It means nothing to me. I do believe, however, that it may have meaning for dogs, hence the term "top dog".

But, getting back to the decision for university, or not, the truth was, in the latter part of my teen years, I was growing up. Always the pragmatist, I now began to feel an urge to interact with the great adventure of Life. University could come later, but first any new learning would consist of on-the-job study relevant to a career in electronics, while using my hands to make tangible inroads into the technological world.

My working life began reasonably well. Fellow teenagers who started with me at a large government international radio station complex were all part-geeks, just like me, and steeped in electronics, just like me. We had a lot in common and we were all good friends even though they were neurotypicals and I was an Aspie.

I suppose there has to be one bad apple. A mid-twenties senior staff member bullied me. My "crime" was that I refused to play his social interaction game. His idea of "normal" was that a man should be aggressive, love rugby and guns, and have a foul mouth. No one was allowed to be different. There was no escape. Eventually my latent nervousness coupled with an inability to understand his reasoning meant I had to resign for my peace of mind. This effectively wrecked a great career path. It was to be about 22 years before I struck another similar bully in an otherwise wonderful job. And then, strangely, another 22 years were to go by, and ditto. In between putting up with those few persons with such intolerant viewpoints, I had some wonderful jobs with wonderful workmates.

Possibly, the electronics field attracts mostly Aspies and geeks. These are related types of personality, in my opinion. Good, sincere people with narrowly focused views, just the type I can relate well to. So mostly, in my working life, I felt as though I fitted in reasonably well with the usual social conditions of my employment. Besides, the hands-on work in electronics was very satisfying for me.

That is, up until this stage of my life. After my diagnosis of AS last year, I finally made the decision for university.

In my teens and twenties, I was painfully shy, as I thought, around women. After all, why would any girl want to be seen with a boy who was different, who liked his own company, and who largely did not mind that state of affairs? Besides, my complete innocence regarding social cues was enough sometimes to have me wondering what had gone wrong this time!

But, social stumbler or not, I dated some attractive young ladies, and at the age of 28, I married.

What an education that was for both of us. Only now, years later, can I look back and see how my Aspie misunderstandings and inabilities caused us some problems. If only one could turn back the clock!

There were several reasons this marriage failed, not all to do with me. It would have helped so much if I had known about my Asperger syndrome earlier on in my life.

To get myself over this failed marriage, I threw myself into the most fearful things I could think of, ballroom dancing and amateur acting. Hobbies where I could be watched all the time were particularly scary. The scarier the better. I wanted the challenge of overcoming terror to help me find the strength of character to carry on with my life in the neurotypical world I thought was my only choice to belong in.

These interests eventually led me to my second wife, who, like me, had taken to dancing and theatre to get over her own broken marriage. After five years of a wonderful relationship, at the age of 40, I popped the question.

To this day I do not know what I did wrong, or what it was I suddenly wasn't doing right after five years, but almost overnight my lovely girlfriend, in my perception, turned into a shocking stranger whose favourite pastime was putting me down in front of our wide circle of friends. Unlike my first marriage, I believe I can lay claim to being the innocent party in this one. After a couple of months of unrelenting put-downs and public insults, I walked out. In 1988 I was single again.

That rather crushed my ambition for anything much, for quite a long time. Eventually, in 1994, I had regained sufficient emotional strength to make a major move to the city of Christchurch on the South Island of New Zealand. Suffice to say, the 14 years to 2008, when my AS was formally confirmed, were a microcosm of my adult life before my move to Christchurch. Nothing new here.

Friends tell me my diagnosis in 2008 appeared to light a fire in me. Apparently I perked up and became a more dynamic person. For me, this revelation of AS feels like nothing has changed yet everything is different. Everything, all of a sudden, makes sense.

The Ugly Duckling is now a swan. To continue the metaphor, I no longer need to battle against a perceived low self-esteem because I cannot understand the behaviour of ducks. Instead, I look for fellow swans, a much more enriching use of my energies.

And so, powered up, full steam ahead as is my wont – that is, when something interests me, I typically go at things full on, no half measures – I enrolled at the University of Canterbury in Christchurch.

The Disability Centre at the university is a highly supportive institution. There is great understanding at this university of the needs of AS people, and much more. The friendly interview covered all the help they could offer me. For me, it was things like being told of the special quiet areas in the main university library. For solitary study, very important to some of us, there are locked quiet rooms available. Aspies need to ask for a key. Healthy neurotypicals are refused a key.

At my assent, the Heads of School relevant to my studies were to be privately told of my AS. The semester, just finished as I write, has demonstrated to me that this translates into a competent and friendly student/tutor relationship for Aspies, in the tutorials at least.

My intention is to aim for a BA, majoring in psychology. The fascinating thing about the introductory psychology lectures is that, unbeknownst to four of us who gravitated to sitting next to each other over time, three eventually admitted to brain damage due to accidents and I was the Aspie in the group. I wonder how we four knew that we were differently wired to the neurotypicals in the room and therefore there was a certain kind of bond causing us to sit together. Maybe it was coincidence...maybe.

I soon discovered the importance of quiet or familiar surroundings when I needed to study. As soon as lectures or tutorials were over for the day, I returned home, close by. Were I living a long way from the university, or if I knew I was returning to a noisy home, I would probably have felt the need to study in one of the quiet rooms on campus and lock myself in. I am so easily distracted by others. Even if someone nearby is not noisy,

I feel imposed upon by people close by and it interferes with my peace of mind.

To anyone who is blessed with AS, I encourage you, if you want to go to university, then go. First, you will have help offered by the faculty if needed, and with a smile. There is not the slightest hint of being embarrassed or being disadvantaged either by lecturer or circumstance.

Second, unlike the terror through ignorance I felt at being trapped among unfathomable neurotypical students when I was contemplating university in 1964, after these many years I have discovered that the students I speak with today are helpful and non-judgemental. Perhaps that is because I have a better understanding of my syndrome now. If I carefully plan my "ad lib" conversations, perhaps I won't repeat myself too many times compared to a neurotypical.

Or it could be that I am so many decades older than the other students that I could never fit into their social circles anyway. Therefore I do not have to try, which in turn means that there is no fear of a perceived rejection without understanding why, like sometimes happened in the old days.

The knowledge that I am blessed with Asperger syndrome proves to be more liberating as my life continues to progress. I proudly tell everybody that I have it. Sometimes I even play a joke on the neurotypicals: I look them up and down with a mock disparaging look on my face, and say with a mock sneer, "Neurotypicals!", followed by "Ptooey!" (mock spit on the ground). You will be amazed how small a sense of humour many neurotypicals can have.

Born in Wanganui, Stan now lives in Christchurch, New Zealand. As a young boy he discovered science books, and electronics as a teen, combining these into a career and hobby for over 50 years. Officially diagnosed in 2008, Stan finally understands himself. In 2009 Stan became a university student, studying psychology.

CHAPTER 3

STUDYING THROUGH DIAGNOSIS

Iain Payne

I always knew that I was different from others. This view was reinforced constantly throughout my childhood and indeed beyond. I observed other people interacting with each other and making friends and wanted to be like them; however, it wasn't easy. In fact, it was a bit like trying to nail jelly to the ceiling. I would spend hours observing them trying to work out the rules they followed. I would then copy these rules and try to emulate people. Without fail I was unsuccessful. I would be met with ridicule and laughter at best, or hostility and threats at worst. Often people would call me stupid or mad, which puzzled me, as I knew I was neither. After many years of this treatment I gradually started to believe what people were saying. There is also nothing worse than trying to make friends with people and to be constantly rejected. My parents didn't understand my behaviour or me. At times I felt I didn't belong to my parents and that I must have been adopted because I was so very different from them. I also believe my brother, who is three years younger than myself, was embarrassed by me at school.

I always tended to be anxious around people, as I didn't understand them. People were unpredictable, inconsistent and quite often very mean to me. The latter being especially unfathomable. I was always trying to help other people, but people rarely seemed grateful. I would become anxious when surrounded by people. I wouldn't be able to predict what they would do next. I increasingly felt that they were in a pack and I was their prey. From everything I saw of them, it was obvious that I was very different from them indeed. Sometimes a group of people would become aggressive towards me. Possibly because they realised that I was different or they misinterpreted my body language.

Whilst surrounded by people I would often find it so overwhelming that I would have a need to escape. Obviously this made working in a job problematic. If I couldn't get away, my anxiety would increase and I would often have a panic attack. Later I developed a way of coping within crowds of people. I would remove myself mentally from the situation, if it weren't possible to do so physically. I would disassociate. It would be like an invisible barrier around me. The noise would fade away and I would feel calmer. However, this strategy meant that I would be less aware of my surroundings and wouldn't be responsive to anything. Often I would have mental absences. I would lose time. I would literally lose minutes at a time. Sometimes people would ask me if I was OK; usually, however, they would just look at me in a strange way.

Previously, as a child, there had been investigations carried out by a neurologist to find out if I was epileptic, due to my disassociating appearing to be Petit Mal, a form of childhood epilepsy characterised by impairment of consciousness, which seemed to match my symptoms. As I got older these episodes became less frequent, as I learnt not to withdraw as completely. This still means though that I sometimes don't realise immediately when someone is talking to me. I can also have trouble when confronted with angry people. I find that I can't stand up for myself as my thinking seems to slow down and I disassociate myself from the situation.

By the time I reached 26 I was in despair. I couldn't relate to other people and I had been in a series of dead-end jobs. I was then working as a chef in a restaurant. One thing I did notice whilst I was there was that I tended to get on better with the university students who worked there part-time than with my co-workers. I think that the students were shocked that I was as intelligent as they were and knew what they were talking about. I even helped one of them with their university assignment. One of the students suggested that I should go to college or university. I subsequently started an Open University course, which I enjoyed immensely.

Unfortunately, due to a lack of friendships and healthy social interactions, I then began to suffer from depression. I felt that there was nothing I could do about my situation and yet couldn't be bothered to do anything about it. I became lethargic and felt tired all of the time. For a while I resisted seeking help because I was worried about the stigma of being labelled mentally ill. I thought it would mean that it would be impossible to get a job in the future. When I started to consider suicide more and more, I knew that I would have to get help. I went to see my doctor who said he would refer me to a mental health professional.

I saw a number of psychologists and psychiatrists over a short time period. Only one of them had a rough idea about what was wrong with me. The others came up with such a large range of diagnoses that they covered pretty much every mental illness between them. When I read *The Bell Jar* by Sylvia Plath later I recognised her metaphor perfectly. Many years later I discovered that "reality is subjective, not objective". There are in fact many different world-views, all equally valid.

One psychiatrist tried to provoke me by shouting at me. When this had no effect, she became interested in my love life. Up to this point I'd had few relationships with women and many bad experiences. She then suggested that I was gay and should come to terms with it and when I learnt to accept this I would be cured. I was certainly not gay; perhaps my fuchsia-coloured shirt confused her?

Finally another psychiatrist did conclude that I had a developmental disorder akin to autism, but it couldn't be autism as I was an adult of normal IQ. According to him, only children with low IQs were autistic! Mind you, he also told me that I had a number of personality disorders, but wouldn't specify which ones in particular. He also said that he could not find a cause for my depression so it may be a chemical imbalance. It was plain to me that the cause was in fact my constant rejection and hostility from other people, not to mention constantly being told that I was stupid and mad. All of this had the potential to make my problems worse, not better. I was in effect having the views of people confirmed by these so-called experts. Luckily I still had some self-belief and knew that they were wrong about me. I was prescribed anti-depressants and was sent to a support group for social phobic people. I soon realised that I was very different from the other people there. Many of them were social phobic and had anxiety problems. OK, the anxiety problems I could identify with, but I knew that I wasn't in any way social phobic.

After I had done a few Psychology courses with the Open University, I thought about doing a full-time degree. I found out that I could get a grant if I went to university and this was about the same as my wages. Thus at the age of 30 I found myself at university studying Psychology and Health. I chose Psychology in order to try and find out what was wrong with me once and for all. I spent much of my time at university trying to fit in with the other students. I spent a lot of time helping other students with their work. I didn't work as hard as I could have done, but still ended up with a 2.1 BSc (Hons). At last it was official: I wasn't stupid! My studies hadn't really helped with my quest for an answer, but I did recognise that some of my symptoms were similar to autism.

A few years after graduating I read *Nobody Nowhere* by Donna Williams, an autobiography by an autistic woman. I recognised many of her experiences. I emailed her and we exchanged several emails. This pointed me in the direction of autism.

I soon realised that my symptoms and world-view most closely matched Asperger syndrome. At last it all made sense. I used the internet to research all I could about AS. Everything I read about it confirmed that I had it. I joined several email lists for people with AS and soon met people I could understand and relate to. There still remained the problem of a formal diagnosis though. I contacted the UK National Autistic Society by email and wrote about my experiences. I soon received a nice reply stating that I indeed was extremely likely to have AS. I haven't had a formal diagnosis yet, but I don't believe I really need one. I now know why I am different.

When I was in my late twenties I finally met a woman who understood me, Brenda, and we fell in love and married. I didn't tell her about my previous dealings with mental health professionals. She is neurotypical and this has caused a number of communication problems between us. Mind you, I have learnt a lot about neurotypical behaviour from her. Brenda had supported my decision to go to Bath Spa University College a year after we were married, and offered encouragement to me throughout my time there.

My wife, being gregarious, now understands me better since my diagnosis. She accepts my need for solitude at times and my dislike of crowds. She no longer thinks that I am being rude or antisocial if I need to escape from family gatherings or social occasions with friends in our home.

I am now more aware of my differences from neurotypical people. I have learnt more about body language than I ever thought I would. I can even do the eyebrow greeting flash. Mind you, I have to do it consciously and I feel very silly doing it. People do seem to like it though! I have learnt to pace myself when dealing with people. I still find being in a group of people stressful and exhausting though. I need to have time on my own to recharge my batteries. Sometimes I am overwhelmed by external reality. I become overloaded with information and have trouble separating out what I should be attending to. This means that I can often miss important things happening around me or I'll forget to do something. My mind tends to wander as well. I am also more aware of my tendency towards obsessive behaviour.

One thing that neurotypical people don't seem to understand is that autistics need routine and structure. The key point, I believe, is the need for predictability in an often unpredictable and confusing world. This is also linked to a resistance to change. The problem is that situations often need a flexible response. Often I find that if I have enough time to weigh up the options and alternatives for action, I usually am able to make the right choice. The problem occurs when I have only a short time to make a decision. If pushed for a response I will invariably go for the wrong option.

There are many advantages to having AS. Such as, I can focus on an issue without getting distracted from it, I am not interested in status or power and I can also see both sides of an argument without becoming emotional.

I am happier now that I know why I am different from most people and I now know my strengths and weaknesses, and I don't have to try to be someone I'm not.

Iain was born in 1963, in Somerset, UK. His father worked as a lecturer with the Army and his mother was a housewife. When Iain was 29 he had the opportunity to go to university and graduated in 1997. At the age of 36 he discovered that he had AS.

PART 2

CAREERS

The five contributors in this section communicate how finding the right career path benefits not only the person with ASD but also the community.

A goal may be to turn their childhood obsession into a career – computer programmer, engineer, actor, researcher, etc. If the position relates to their special interest they may be less likely to become bored or stressed. They may thrive on repetition, attention to detail, and working individually rather than with a team.

Once again finding the strengths and abilities of a person with ASD and channelling them into their working environment can have very positive outcomes.

- *Temple Grandin* not only helps other individuals with true "Aspie" advice on employment, but also discloses the keys to her successful career.

- *Roger N. Meyer* reports how counselling affects those diagnosed with Asperger late in life, and how he, the counselled, became the counsellor.

- *Damian Santomauro* converses with us on the life experiences that were his stepping-stones to his future career.

- *Malcolm Johnson* reveals how the characteristics of Asperger syndrome are the key elements of his success in management and leadership.

- *Sondra Williams* points out how her strengths, in particular her ability to focus, assist her to function within the community as a speaker on the topic of autism and to apply her skills to various autism groups.

CHAPTER 4

TALENTED PEOPLE GETTING EMPLOYED

FACTORS THAT HELP INDIVIDUALS ON THE AUTISM/ASPERGER SPECTRUM GET GOOD EMPLOYMENT AND CAREERS

Temple Grandin, PhD

Photograph by Rosalie Winard

People on the autism spectrum often have uneven skills. They will have an area of strength and an area of weakness. I'm a visual thinker and all my thoughts are in pictures. My weak area is algebra because there is nothing to visualize. Visual thinkers like me are good at jobs such as graphic design, drafting, industrial design, and photography. Other individuals on the autism/Asperger spectrum may be music and math thinkers or word fact thinkers. The music and math minds think in patterns and they often excel at music, engineering, computer programming, and math. The word fact thinkers can memorize hundreds of facts. Some of these individuals may be good at journalism, library science, or special education. They are not visual thinkers.

To be successful in the world of employment and have a real career, success is more likely if the job requires use of the individual's area of strength. Being a visual thinker is a great asset for an equipment designer. When I design a livestock facility, I can test run it in my mind like a 3D virtual-reality computer system. When I was in my twenties, I did not know that many other people did not think in pictures. I assumed that other people's thoughts were the same as mine. When I wrote *Thinking in Pictures*, I interviewed many people about how they think, which gave me great insight into how my mind worked.

TALENTED PEOPLE NOT GETTING EMPLOYED

I am dismayed at the number of smart people in the autism/ Asperger spectrum who are not able to obtain and keep good jobs that can become real careers. At the age of 64, I am realizing that my old-fashioned 1950s upbringing gave me skills that really helped me in the workplace. In my early childhood, I was taught how to take turns with board games. I had to learn how to wait my turn. The things that were fun in the fifties had to be done with another child. Another thing that really helped me was being taught the importance of having good manners. I was taught to say *please* and *thank you* and I was praised and rewarded when I did tasks that pleased another person. The work ethic was taught from an early age. When I was nine years old, I volunteered to sew costumes for the school plays on my toy hand-cranked sewing machine. I enjoyed the praise and recognition I received. When I was 13, my mother had me work two afternoons a week for a seamstress who worked out of her home. Throughout childhood, my interests and abilities in art were always encouraged.

Talent should be developed. An obsessive talent can often turn into a career. If a child always draws the same cartoon characters, broaden his/her skills by asking for a drawing of the character's house or car. Use the motivation of special interests to develop a career – but the individual has to learn how to do projects that are assigned to them.

I had a lot of problems in high school and I was a terrible student. But throughout my high school years I was always making and building things that pleased other people. Even though I seldom studied or did homework, I did lots of projects for other people, such as building gates, painting signs, making scenery for the high school play, and shingling the barn roof.

Both in high school and college, mother realized that she had to get me out during the summer doing different things and working. When I was 16, I visited my aunt's ranch in Arizona, and that is where my interest in cattle started. At first I was reluctant to go to the ranch because the idea of going to a new place made me nervous and I would miss my favorite TV shows. Mother gave me two choices – go to the ranch and come home in two weeks or stay all summer. I ended up staying all summer. She was right to get me out to the ranch. Like many people on the spectrum, I had to be pushed to try new things. When I was in college, I continued to visit the ranch during the summer but mother and the counselor at my college set up two summer internships. One summer I worked in a research lab and the other I worked with autistic children. Getting the work experience *before* I graduated from college helped me to be successful. Today I am seeing too many people on the spectrum graduating from college with no work experience. They should be getting work experience while they are still in high school and college.

It is never too late to start working on learning a career. Even in my later years, from 55 to 60, I am still learning. The 30-year-old who has no work experience can still learn how to do a job. I had to be pushed to go out to the ranch, and an older person may need lots of encouragement to do something new. I am amazed at how much I have developed and learned in my forties and fifties. Other people tell me that my social skills at 60 are better than they were when I was 50.

MENTORS

Why was I so industrious making scenery for the school play and such a slacker goofing off with my high school studies? I could see no goal for studying. My high school academic career turned around when I started working with Mr. Carlock, my science teacher. He took my obsession with my squeezing machine and used it to motivate studying. He told me that to discover why deep pressure was so relaxing, I had to learn how to search the scientific literature and go to college. Now studying had a concrete goal that I could understand, and I started studying. In college I got all As and Bs except in French class. Fortunately in the sixties, college math was not algebra but finite math, which was more concrete, and I learned about probability and matrices. Mr. Don, the kind math teacher, tutored me after many of the classes. I am observing that there is a subset of individuals on the spectrum who can do geometry and trigonometry but they cannot do algebra. I never had the opportunity to try geometry because I kept failing algebra through there being nothing to visualize. Some students need to skip algebra and do other forms of higher math.

MAKE A PORTFOLIO OF YOUR WORK

I had to sell my work and not myself. To sell clients my livestock equipment designs, I made portfolios of photos and drawings. People thought I was weird, but they respected me when they saw my work. An effective portfolio should contain your best work. The work you choose to put in it should be appropriate for the employer you are sending it to. Elaborate science fiction art is not going to impress an advertising agency that does ads for banks. Some beautiful logos for fictitious companies would be more appropriate. Do not put too much stuff in your portfolio. It should contain only five or ten pages showing your best work. It must be neatly presented so the reader instantly thinks, "This guy has talent." Some of the items that should be put in the portfolio are drawings, artwork, computer code, test scores, photos, or samples of writing. Each page should show a different example of your work.

I am appalled at the amount of emails and letters I get that do not contain complete contact information. You have to make it easy for a busy person to contact you. Contact information should include email, all your phone numbers, and your postal address. Sometimes it is best to send the portfolios in the old-fashioned postal mail. Many people will not open email attachments from strangers. There is more information on making portfolios in my book *Developing Talents*.

During interviews, I made a poor impression and my portfolio saved me from getting fired. Early in my career, I wrote articles for a farm magazine called *The Arizona Farmer Ranchman*. When the magazine was sold, we got a new boss who thought I was weird. Fortunately my friend Susan, who did the page layouts, saw the subtle social warning signs that Jim did not like me. She told me to make a portfolio of all my articles. When Jim saw how much good work I had done, he gave me a raise.

FIND THE BACK DOOR

When I was in my twenties, I figured out how to find the people who would open the back door for me. Often a job works out best if a sympathetic person just lets you try it. The way I got into a well-known meat plant in Arizona to start my career was a chance meeting with the right person. At an Arizona cattle meeting I met the wife of the plant's insurance agent. She was impressed with my hand-embroidered western shirt. I was wearing my portfolio but I did not realize it at the time. People respect talent and she saw my abilities in my shirt. Back doors are everywhere, you just have to be creative and find them.

HOW MUCH MUST YOU CONFORM?

There is a lot of discussion in the autism/Asperger community on how much you should have to conform to society's norms. Basic good manners are essential. When I started a job with a feedlot construction company, I was a slob and I wore work uniforms. My new boss forced me to make some changes. He told me that he respected my intellect but I had to start wearing deodorant and dress better. At the time I was furious, but today I thank him. What ended up happening was a compromise. I cleaned up my hygiene, but I still wear western attire, which is unconventional. It is perfectly fine to be eccentric but you must not be a filthy, rude slob.

I met a really great Aspie who teaches a college course in astronomy. Every day he wears a different really cool astronomy t-shirt and his beautiful long ponytail. His ponytail was neat and clean and it expressed his individuality. I told him to never let anybody make him cut it off and that it was really wonderful that he was neat, clean, and polite.

RELATIONSHIPS WITH CO-WORKERS

I did not understand how the chain of command works in a corporation. Your boss will get really upset if you go over his head. In the 1970s I was fired from an equipment company because I reported engineering mistakes on a project to the president of the company instead of reporting to my boss at the equipment company. I was right from a technical standpoint but socially wrong. I then switched to freelance work, which solved a lot of problems. I went into the plant, designed and supervised installation of the equipment and then I left. Freelance makes the rules simpler. My rule for freelance work was always report to the individual who hired me unless the project is in danger of failure. The only time you go over your client's head is to save the project. I call it being project loyal.

Another thing I had to learn is to not tell other people they are stupid even if they are stupid. I had to learn diplomacy. If a colleague makes a mistake, I may say, "You did a good job on this part of the project but I can show you a better way to do the other part."

JEALOUS CO-WORKERS

One of the most difficult things I had to deal with was jealous people who sabotaged my equipment. The plant manager would hire me to design a new system, but the resident plant engineer did not like this nerd invading his turf. In three different plants I had actual physical damage done to conveyors. In one plant, a meat hook was jammed in a conveyor when I left the room for a few minutes. When I first started working, I naively assumed that everybody who worked in a company would always have their employer's best interests in mind. It was a shock for me to learn that this is not always the case. Today I have learned that the best way to deal with a jealous colleague is to ask his advice for help on the project. Pull him in and ask him for assistance in an area where he has talent. On one job, the plant engineer was upset because we had to tear out the hydraulic system that he had installed incorrectly. His hydraulic system was awful but his electrical work was really beautiful. I made a big point of complimenting his electrical work. On another project, I was really tactless when I said some sloppy welding was like "pigeon doo doo." The wise old plant engineer made me apologize to the other workers for the crude language. I was not going to compliment his welding because it was terrible, but I told him I was sorry for the rude comments about pigeon doo doo.

To avoid jealousy problems caused by doing quality work too fast, I used to get the drawing done in two days and then wait a week before I sent it to the client. In today's computerized world, it would be really easy to do this. What often happens is that the big bosses will often really like you. When you are hired to design a project or fix the computers, the resident engineering or computer person may really resent you. He feels stupid because you were hired to do a project he could not do. The person who is most likely to hate you is the person who has the same job that you are doing. The plant manager will probably love you and the hourly workers on the line will love you, but the resident engineer feels that his "turf" has been threatened. It's like a dog that growls when you approach because he does not want you invading his "turf."

PROBLEMS WITH BAD BOSSES

There are two kinds of bad bosses. The first type is hated by almost all the employees, and the second type does not get along with the "weird" Aspie. Both normal and Aspie employees often have to find new jobs when the boss is really terrible. If you leave a job, make sure you have kept samples of your work for your portfolio. I heard a sad story about a designer who left a job and the only copies of her work were on an old obsolete unplayable disk.

In some cases the boss may ask you to do something illegal or discriminate against you. You must think very carefully about filing lawsuits. Even though there are laws protecting you, you can get branded as a troublemaker and have difficulty finding a new job. If you are asked to do something criminal or dangerous, it is often the best option to quit. In a really bad situation with an employer, you may have to make a serious life-changing decision. Do I file the lawsuit and dedicate my life to being an activist, or do I continue my career at another more ethical company?

People on the spectrum have lost some excellent jobs by being promoted into management positions that they could not handle. This can happen in any field. An example of a good way to handle this is to say, "I am a techie and please let me do a technical job." I am doing well as a college professor, but I would never want to be an administrator.

CONTROVERSIAL TOPICS AND RUDE TALK

To keep your job, avoid discussing controversial topics such as religion, sex, politics, and race at work. Keep these views to yourself. Talk about safe topics such as sports, pets, favorite TV shows, cooking, hobbies, etc. It's perfectly fine to be a *Star Trek* fan and talk about that, but strong political views are not welcome. One person on the spectrum got fired from a job for racial comments. Leave these topics at home. You may also get into trouble with getting and keeping employment if you write hateful, nasty stuff on websites and listservs. Never post inappropriate pictures on social networking sites such as Facebook. Employees often do internet searches on prospective employees. Be very careful with your employer's computer and phone. Nothing you do on your work computer or phone is private. Anything you write or webpages you surf can be accessed by your boss. You must remember when you type on your work computer, you must always think, how would it look on your boss's computer? If you are angry and upset, use your *personal* phone and leave the computer alone.

When I was a child I learned not to make rude comments about what other people look like. One Aspie with a degree in library science was fired from several libraries for laughing and making comments about fat people in the elevator. I learned when I was eight not to talk this way. When my sister and I were laughing about how my fat aunt's breasts looked like horse feedbags, mother made it very clear that if Aunt Beth heard that talk, we would be punished. At work, just keep your mouth shut about other people's appearance.

CONTROLLING EMOTIONS

In high school, I was kicked out for fighting and throwing a book at a girl who teased me. It is difficult for me to control my emotions. I can be really happy and laugh really loud or be really angry. To control anger, I switched from anger to crying. Instead of fists or throwing things, I cried. In the meat plants,

I hid in the electrical room or went into the cattle stockyard. A violent incident at work will get you fired. I could not control anger so I switched to crying. People who cry can keep jobs. An adult with raging temper tantrums gets fired. At a large software company, a talented Aspie programmer lost his job because he had a screaming tantrum. He threw a fit because the break room had the wrong kind of cookies and snacks. I was taught when I was about nine that if I did not like Granny's cookies that had yucky green things on them, I was to say "No thank you" and make no comments. The employee could have avoided being fired by bringing in snacks from home or politely asking the person who provided the snacks to stock his favorites.

SENSORY SENSITIVITIES

Sound sensitivity and visual sensitivity can be really debilitating and make normal workplaces intolerable. Fluorescent lights are one of the worst issues. Some people on the spectrum can see the 50- to 60-cycle flickers so they feel like they are in a disco nightclub. A lamp with an old-fashioned hot light bulb at your desk will help reduce the flicker. Placing your desk near a window also helps. If fluorescent lights bother your eyes, you may be able to read a laptop computer screen more easily. Laptop screens have no flicker. Some of the flat panel displays are bad because there is a fluorescent light inside which illuminates the screen. When testing out a new screen, use a laptop as a comparison to make sure the new screen does not flicker. Irlen-colored lenses really help some people. If going to Irlen is too expensive, try on lots of different pale pastel-colored glasses at the sunglass store.

If sound hurts your ears, you can wear a music headset or earplugs. To prevent your ears from getting more sensitive, the earplugs must be off for at least half of your waking hours. If a co-worker has a ringtone that bothers you, ask them to change it. These are simple accommodations that will make your work environment more comfortable.

AVOID MULTITASKING, AND ASK FOR CLEAR DEFINITION OF TASKS

Avoid jobs that require multitasking, such as a receptionist, who has to type and answer the phone at the same time. I would be fired on the first day if I had to be a cashier in a busy restaurant. Ask your boss for written instructions so you will remember them. This is especially important for tasks that have multiple steps. In graduate school, I worked in the dairy, milking cows. Fortunately the ten steps for setting up the milkers were on a laminated sign on the wall. I would have been in trouble without this sign because remembering the sequence of the steps was difficult. Ask your boss for clear directions. If you are writing software, ask your boss exactly what he wants the software to do. If he gives you vague instructions, such as "develop new software," ask for more specifics. An example of a specific goal would be design a program where a single click on a desktop icon would bring up a page with a search box for searching all the memory of a user's computer. The page should have tabs labeling everything, Word documents, PowerPoint, spreadsheets, and photos. This program must be simple enough to use so that no instructions would be needed to use it after it is installed. The boss should also give you some technical guidelines on things such as the amount of memory the program can use, but otherwise he should let his Aspie employee figure out how to write the program.

Recently I talked to a freelance architect who has Asperger syndrome. She had problems with arguments with clients over how to design houses. I told her to avoid talking about how to design a house and to direct the conversation to specific design outcomes. Instead of fighting about which styles of architecture are the best, she should start by showing the client a portfolio of other homes she has designed. I do the same thing when I design corrals for cattle. Usually the client will like one of my designs and then I say, "I can design something similar for your ranch." I then ask a few questions about numbers and types of cattle and then I end the conversation about design. I told the Aspie architect that she talked too much about design.

CONCLUSIONS

Having a good career has made my life worthwhile. The happiest adults on the autism/Asperger spectrum have careers they really like. I want to help everyone to find work they will like.

Temple Grandin is Professor of Animal Science at Colorado State University and a designer of livestock handling facilities. She has been featured in the HBO movie Temple Grandin *and has written the bestselling books* Thinking in Pictures *and* Animals' in Translation. *The BBC featured her in the TV documentary "The Woman Who Thinks Like a Cow."*

www.templegrandin.com

CHAPTER 5

COUNSELING THAT WORKS

Roger N. Meyer

Before I was diagnosed at the age of 55 with Asperger syndrome I had spent 20 years in psychotherapy. By the time I finally found a label that fit, I had experienced...

- child and adolescent psychotherapy (Freudian and neo-Freudian)

- non-directive, person-centered psychotherapy

- Gestalt therapy (individual work, encounter groups, group therapy)
- several types of "reality therapy"
- neurolinguistic programming
- Reichian and neo-Reichian therapy
- Rolf Structural Integration (the early seventies "rough stuff")
- milder forms of body manipulation and postural exercises focusing on emotional awareness and mind–body integration
- introductory sessions with a Jungian therapist
- family therapy
- primal scream therapy (the whole nine yards!)
- additional years of psychodynamic individual and group "feel-good" therapy following dramatic crash and burn.

Until my AS diagnosis, not a single thing "stuck."

Having spoken with many other mature, more able, AS adults diagnosed late in life, I've learned that we share more than a common diagnosis. Most of us have similar histories of inadequate counseling. We've encountered widespread counselor arrogance, disbelief, and invalidation. With near unanimity, we agree that traditionally trained mental health professionals have way too much to unlearn and un-think in order to wrap their minds around the phenomenon of AS. Furthermore, many traditionally trained counselors are hung up on *Me Doctor You Patient* and all that this distinction implies.

Most distressing of all, professionals who don't "get" AS protract the counseling relationship with lengthy terminations for their reassurance that it's OK for *them* to say goodbye to us. Many of us already have enough trouble understanding committed relationships. We don't welcome the added baggage of a manufactured attachment disorder built into a counseling package.

Most mature, more able adults diagnosed with AS will agree with this statement:

I am a curious and interested person.

For many of us, two words – *Asperger syndrome* – explain our individual complexity better, but they don't provide answers for... *What's next?*

For "What's next?" we often seek two kinds of answers. Firstly, we seek individualized explanations, explanations that satisfy our craving for personal meaning. These explanations align our new label with our past and present experiences. This *making sense stage* can be quite brief when we find the right kind of help.

Secondly, getting the right diagnosis doesn't stop the merry-go-round. Because we live in an adult world with real adult roles and relationships, we now look for more efficient coping and problem-solving tools to navigate the world of hidden rules relating to them.

Teaching social skills is the mantra of the autism industry. Use of the term *social skills* demeans adults. When I interact with someone the last thing I need to be reminded of is my skill level. If I think "skill," I automatically rank myself in comparison to other people. Because I'm always learning, I'll tend to rank myself lower than others, something that reinforces my fragile sense of self-worth.

This I know: *I don't need any more anxiety.* I'm already aware that I'm "on stage." Why should I flirt with a term that distracts me from readiness to learn how to act more efficiently?

I prefer using the term *identifying and using tools* because people *do* something with tools. What gets me going in any problem-solving situation is the question...

How do I DO this?

I'll get to *Why?* sometime later. Learning new information about relationships and acquiring problem-solving and acting tools equips us to make better choices as we reach forks in the road that face all adults, whether we're on the spectrum or not.

So why hasn't suitable counseling emerged for more able, older AS adults?

One reason: *No Money.* Consumers' cash drives changes in otherwise unresponsive markets. Those of us who can afford counseling present the counseling disciplines with an inadequate critical mass to prompt change. Most AS adults are unemployed, underemployed, and malemployed. Most of us do not have the means to pay for protracted private counseling. We may not need drawn-out work.

What do we want?

Few spectrum-sitting adults, hearing the "A" word for the first time, react with flat affect responses like, "OK, whatever!"

Receiving an AS diagnosis late in life is a life-altering experience. Late diagnosis affects our self-concept, stirring up issues relating to our childhood, adolescence, and adulthood. The older we get, the more apt we are to frame those experiences within a relational perspective, a perspective that in many cases has been dark, a perspective that contributes to our chronic state of low self-esteem. Changing our perspective will not happen by first *thinking* differently. It will happen first by *doing* things differently.

On the surface our issues may appear similar to those of young children, adolescents, or young adults, but they've taken on a qualitative hue different than the pastel colors of youth. Younger persons do not have the kind of wear on their soles (and souls) caused by trudging down the path of mature adult roles, responsibilities, and expectations. Reconsidering our richer life history impacts our selections of diverse new tools used to do things differently in the future.

In my book *Asperger Syndrome Employment Workbook* I outline a process leading up to diagnosis and the aftermath of late-in-life diagnosis. What a few other adult autistic authors and I have begun to address is what older adults are likely to find in the real world – as we seek effective one-to-one personal counseling, if we seek counseling at all.

One reason we may not seek help is that we've conditioned ourselves not to seek it. We may have been disappointed by our past negative counseling experiences.

More to the point, however, is that, for us, personal counseling – as most people think of it – is unaffordable. Furthermore, any counseling that may be affordable still may not suit our needs.

I propose two kinds of counseling experiences that will work for more able late-diagnosed Asperger syndrome adults. Both are based on best practices in adult education. They are cheaper than what is currently on the market. They are founded on respect for diversity and empowering people to become informed problem-solvers and choice makers.

As you shop for counselors immediately following diagnosis, and then as you seek new tools to work personal relationships and solve problems more efficiently, remember these two points...

The first, a warning, applies to a nine-word phrase that counselors could choose *not* to have in their vocabulary or their thinking. That phrase is

***If you'd only try harder, you can do* X*!** (Whatever *X* is)

Those words are toxic. You hear these words from others and from yourself because you long ago internalized "beat me up" language. Those are words you should *never* hear from anyone you've asked only to listen and not give you advice, or when you go to them for coaching and training.

There is a second three-word phrase you *should* expect to hear from a counselor who is as puzzled as you are – maybe more so.

I don't know.

If a counselor cannot say these three words out loud and often and mean them, you haven't found the right person to listen to you.

A NEW COUNSELING PARADIGM
Stage 1 Personal counseling – Talking it out to make sense of the diagnosis

When you finally receive a primary diagnosis of AS you'll go through a post-diagnostic refractory period. If and when you seek personal counseling during this initial period, what you want to find is a person highly skilled in *active listening*. What you'll discover is that there are few professionals equipped to do this work well.

There are more non-counselors who can listen well than there are professionals. A good listener might be a close friend or a relative who accepts you unconditionally.

These folks don't need to know all the terms and concepts used by so-called autism experts. These non-professionals *know you*, and that's often enough to do the trick. Experienced, patient, compassionate lay listeners can listen well. Persons with good pastoral listening skills do this. Don't fret about the person's title. Go for how they listen without judging; how they listen without bursting forth with answers. Coming up with answers is your job, not theirs. People who aren't good listeners often come up with answers because they are uncomfortable with being silent and just allowing you to *be*.

The purpose of this first stage of counseling is not therapy. You're not broken. You may be traumatized, in shock, terribly confused… all of those things, but broken? No. You seek a boost in *translating* your experiences just for yourself. Look for someone to help you make sense of your diagnosis through a *let-me-talk-it-out process*.

You'll know when you're "talked out." The main tip-off is when you start to repeat yourself too often. A good active listener will tell you when you've reached that point. It may take you only a short time to do this, but you'll need the undivided attention of an honest and active listener to get you there. As you talk, your counselor should validate your concerns and feelings without patronizing you. (Many AS folks are especially sensitive to being patronized.)

If you have trouble finding words to express yourself, your counselor can help you find *your own words* without suggesting their words to you.

This first type of post-diagnostic counseling should be short-term but intensive work. Protracting it would only delay getting on with your life. As a mature adult, you should eventually know your life couldn't always be perfect. One thing you can count on, though: it will always be too short.

At the conclusion of this first stage, you should experience a slight sense of tension and positive anticipation about "What's next?" *What's next is what's now...* your continued immersion in adult life, this time with a changed perspective. Determine to spend some time experiencing your AS in the real-world environment before immediately hunting for help of a different kind.

Stage 2 Personal counseling – Acquiring new tools and refurbishing old ones

Training/coaching

For this second stage of counseling, you've identified concrete problems in your day-to-day life. You've always had them, but now you want to deal with them. You have trouble at work, problems with your family, a temper you must handle, money management challenges, trouble knowing how to be assertive without being overbearing, trouble relaxing, and sensory issues that can be tamed.

You now know you must unlearn habits that don't work well or at all, and formally learn things you don't grasp intuitively. There are acting coaches, voice coaches, and adult leisure and recreation trainers out there who don't cost a bundle. Competition is fierce. It's a buyer's market. A bargain-hunter's tip: look for folks who use alternative means to make themselves known. If they're original thinkers, they're likely to be more like you. Look for folks who relish teaching others to do things for themselves.

To start out, you need to feel sure enough of yourself with a person with special abilities to teach a klutz like you how to appear graceful when inside you may still feel like a rubber-legged fool. What you'll likely first learn is how to do something and *how to fake looking natural* doing it. With enough repetition, you'll learn what things you can handle, and what other things aren't worth the personal cost to you to pursue. That's OK. Let them go.

Two final rules

Here are two rules guaranteed to protect you from defective training. *First rule*: If something still feels stupid after you've repeated it many times, and other people tell you it's stupid, it probably *is* stupid. *Second rule*: Trust your gut, not your heart, and never your head if something's consistently not right. It's OK to walk away from a defective trainer or an uncomfortable scene. In fact, you'd be a fool not to.

Results-oriented people recognize the value of keeping things simple. Whenever I present this affordable model of adult counseling to a mixed audience of AS individuals and professionals, they agree that it makes sense. As a lay counselor and autism consultant, I am a firm believer in whatever works. This approach works.

Roger N. Meyer lives in Gresham, Oregon. Author of Asperger Syndrome Employment Workbook *(2001), he founded the Portland AS Support Group in 1998. He co-facilitates the Portland AS Partners group, co-moderates a monthly multidisciplinary AS clinical study group and is president of his Neighborhood Association and Gresham's Coalition of Neighborhood Associations.*

www.rogernmeyer.com

CHAPTER 6

TO BE OR NOT TO BE

Damian Santomauro

It is a common belief that as Asperger syndrome is classified as a disability, it has a purely negative effect on people's lives. Contrary to this belief, Asperger syndrome has given me both challenges and rewards. Every challenge beaten can make you a better person, and so I believe having Asperger syndrome has made me a better person. These challenges have also inspired me to enter a career in psychology helping others with Asperger syndrome, which will make my life very rewarding. However, these challenges would have been more difficult to overcome had I not received early intervention.

I was fortunate enough to obtain a diagnosis at the age of five, and received copious social skills training and behavioural therapy as a child. I frequently met with a speech pathologist and attended part time at a special school for autism spectrum disorders. I was also fortunate to grow up with a very supportive family. My mother would always seek ways to help me through my challenges, and yet she would also teach me to be independent, which I believe was very important, as now I am able to function independently as an adult.

I also observed my peers in school to learn how to be socially acceptable. I realised I was very different to my peers and was always curious as to how they interacted with each other. I would actually study them like a scientist. When social opportunities arose, I would trial what I had learned from watching my peers, and analyse the outcome. I would play these scenarios in my mind hundreds of times, picking apart every little detail, and I would be very critical of myself. I wanted to be accepted, and I wanted to be a "normal" child.

My studies of human behaviour continued into high school. By this stage my investigations began to dominate my adolescence. "Why did she say this? Why did he do that?" My school life was full of these questions. I dedicated my entire adolescence to investigating the social system and perfecting it for myself to seem socially acceptable. I even sacrificed academic effort for this. However, the amount of effort I put into my social investigations seem to have paid off in the end, as now people find it difficult to believe I have Asperger syndrome. I am quite proud to know I have made such progress in my social skills. These new social skills came with many benefits, opening many new doors for me in the social world. It exposed me to understanding humour, social outings, partying with my peers, and friendships. Unfortunately, however, my obsession with becoming a "normal" person had also changed who I was, and had caused me great pain. I experienced rejection, rivalry, heartbreak, and great dissatisfaction in life. I believed that if I would become an accepted and "normal" person that I would be a happy person. This was not the case, however, and these realisations led me to the darkest time of my life during my final year of high school.

I had worked so hard, and endured much stress and anxiety to become a normal person, and yet I felt no happier. This led me to hold much resentment and hatred towards individuals without Asperger syndrome, as I felt I had to change to suit "their" world. I also held a jealousy for what I considered as them having a relatively easier life than I had (at least in regard to social acceptance). I also felt severely depressed as I felt that if being "normal" would not make me happy, then there was nothing life could offer that would ever make me happy. This cocktail of emotions erupted into suicidal and homicidal thoughts and intentions. These thoughts and intentions grew so strongly that I was admitted to hospital in the adolescent mental health unit.

I remember feeling quite disappointed with the hospital process and staff. I felt the mental health staff were quite ignorant of my situation, and failed to understand my problems. Once I was talking to the head psychiatrist about my suicidal intentions, and rather than listening, she began an argument with me on the subject. I for one felt there was no reason to argue, and also felt there was no reason to talk to someone who was not listening to me, so I stopped talking. Following this discussion, the psychiatrist told my parents that she had "conquered me" and had changed my attitudes towards committing suicide. Truth of the matter was I saw no point in talking to her. I had not changed my attitudes on suicide. I was still a severe suicide risk, and I was quite fortunate that she was not the decision maker on when I was to be released from hospital. Following discharge from the hospital, another psychiatrist monitored me. Unfortunately, this psychiatrist seemed more interested in the weather than any issues I disclosed.

Also, this psychiatrist was a prescription dispenser; all he did was prescribe anti-depressants. Though my overall experience with the mental health system was quite negative, it had a significant positive outcome for me. It inspired me to help improve the mental health system for individuals with autism spectrum disorders. A few months after I was released from hospital, my mother asked me to accompany her to an international autism conference in South Africa. Here I was exposed to a multitude of psychology professions researching and presenting information to help individuals with autism spectrum disorders. It was here that I realised I wanted a career in psychology. It is quite interesting that, after a life observing and analysing human behaviour for social understanding, I would choose a field of science that is dedicated to researching human behaviour. Had it not been for my diagnosis of Asperger syndrome, I never would have felt the need to conduct these observations. I would never have gone to hospital and I would never have attended the autism conference in South Africa.

Before I even decided to choose a career in psychology, I was already helping those with Asperger syndrome. At the age of 15 I spoke on panels with other teenagers with Asperger syndrome in front of large audiences. Eventually I was speaking on the topic of Asperger syndrome independently at national seminars and conferences. These conference talks have helped me build my reputation in my chosen career field in psychology. Another contribution to my career is having a self-help book for teenagers with Asperger syndrome published, which I co-wrote with my mother. We wrote this book to help other teenagers with Asperger syndrome.

If they have a question or an issue, they can look it up in the book and read information and advice on that topic. The book includes my experiences, and I am hoping readers can learn from my mistakes, instead of making mistakes of their own. This was published and distributed internationally, and I am still in disbelief about the fact that I am now a published international author! To already have a published book in the same field as my future career is very helpful. I had also gained experience in helping to facilitate a workshop for children with autism spectrum disorders. My mother and a family friend, Dr Margaret Carter, ran a workshop for young boys with Asperger syndrome. I was offered a chance to assist them. I found I was able to relate to the boys a lot, and many of them reminded me of myself when I was their age. It further inspired me to help individuals with autism spectrum disorders, and it gave me hope for their future. If they were like me when I was their age, then there was a good chance that with help they could develop into successful and independent individuals like myself.

These earlier contributions to my career and my own experiences of Asperger syndrome have helped me choose and develop my career in psychology. I have just completed my honours degree in psychology, and my thesis was investigating whether individuals with Asperger syndrome have a different concept of ownership of property to individuals without Asperger syndrome. I have now enrolled in a doctorate of philosophy in psychology, researching emotion regulation in adolescents with autism spectrum disorders. I believe my personal experience with Asperger syndrome will benefit my clients as a clinical psychologist, or my research as an academic researcher. Both careers have positive contributions to the field of psychology in autism spectrum disorders. In five years' time, I see myself either practising as a clinical psychologist, working with individuals with autism spectrum disorders, or performing postdoctoral research on autism spectrum disorders – but I tend to be favouring the latter. These career pathways take much time and dedication, but I believe it will have a very rewarding outcome. I will be working in a profession that I am passionate about, and if it were not for my diagnosis of Asperger syndrome when I was five, I would probably not have chosen this career pathway. Nowadays I hear of many children with Asperger syndrome going through what I went through, and I am very motivated to help them and to make their lives easier. This will be my contribution in life, and this will be a rewarding one of Aspies helping Aspies.

Damian was diagnosed with Asperger at the age of five. Now at the age of 22 he has successfully completed his Honours in Psychology and is studying for his PhD researching Asperger syndrome. Damian enjoys watching sci-fi, riding his motorcycle, and of course eating traditional Italian food!

CHAPTER 7

SUCCESSFUL MANAGEMENT – SAVANT STYLE

Malcolm Johnson

There is always much publicity about the barriers to success that having Asperger syndrome (AS) confers, but very little about the benefits. However, there are many, and some are extraordinarily useful in management positions. Indeed, they have contributed significantly to my managerial success.

Much has been made recently about the special, "savant" skills that certain people affected by AS are thought to possess. The highest profile personality from a business perspective is Bill Gates, who is widely thought to be affected by the condition to some degree. Without doubt, Bill Gates possesses extraordinary business talents. The ability to write groundbreaking software is driven – possibly – by the logical mode of thought and the insight that his cognitive skills deliver.

Key for me is my insight and my ability to "think outside of the box". My mind thinks differently, and this offers tremendous advantages. In particular, I am highly analytical and can appraise business scenarios very effectively. This means I am able to identify not only the key dynamics impacting upon a business quickly, but I can also see the wider picture.

Strategically this is invaluable. Today, too much time and effort in business is, I believe, expended in dealing with day-to-day issues and micro-managing. That is fine, provided a company or department is on the right track. If it is not, however, then difficulties soon appear and can even be terminal commercially.

I have always been able to see the wider picture and the implications of it. I enjoy – and am highly adept at – looking at different market scenarios and identifying where it is going and what a company strategically needs to do. I used to think that most managers could do this. As I have gone through my career, however, I have very quickly come to appreciate that they cannot, and this is a fundamental commercial shortcoming. In today's business environment, it is perhaps the most important thing of all. Markets change so fast and with unpredictability in the digital world that failure to spot the trend early can have catastrophic consequences. This different insight is often unique and possibly due to my literal mode of thinking.

I like and focus on facts and not opinion. I identify the facts or key drivers quickly, assimilate them and then place them in the overall context of a market.

My MBA training has assisted the process enormously by giving me the analytical tools. However, without the ability to view and process the data, I would be unable to place it within the academic framework. This ability has led to a number of successes. I formulated a strategy for a multi-media division in the BBC; a strategy for a professional services network; and, in my current role, a marketing strategy for entry into the online games market.

In each case, the market was being subjected to, and was influenced by, enormous, rapid change. In the online games market, for example, the digital process is enhancing the product development process and leading to ever more sophisticated products; but many of the latter are "me too" and demonstrate no point of differentiation. A new market segment needed to be attacked, and my mindset, and the business training the MBA afforded, enabled me to identify a middle path, one that appeals to mainstream and casual gamers alike – and one which also was vastly more effective to develop for.

Allied to an analytical mode of thought is my higher than average IQ. Though I do not regard myself as having an exceptional intellect, the three degrees I have do suggest that I am above average intelligence, probably more so than most managers. For me, success in business does not depend solely on intellect. However, it does help and enables me to think deeper about issues and where a decision may be leading.

Another key factor that has contributed towards my success in business has been my integrity. Like everyone else with AS I demonstrate a high degree of honesty, integrity and trustworthiness. But it hasn't always been automatically advantageous; indeed at times, my tendency to be too open has caused setbacks. However, overall it has been beneficial. People trust me. After a time they can sense my honesty and high integrity levels and so feel able to discuss openly and frankly with me issues that may otherwise be contentious with other managers. For superiors and fellow managers, it has proved to be an enormous asset. I don't play games or indulge in corporate politics. I am straight with people, they know that, something that they appreciate, which, in turn, generates reciprocal loyalty. In the long term this is not only invaluable but becomes self-strengthening. The more people trust me, the more I am sounded out…and the more influence I can exert. Moreover, I enjoy the faith that people show in me and their willingness to confide personal or contentious issues.

This factor is prevalent in my current role. Sensing that I was honest and in possession of a high level of integrity was instrumental in securing my position in the online games company. In turn, this has strengthened my standing within the company going forward. My boss confides in me sensitive issues and asks for my insight and opinion. This, in turn, generates support and loyalty from him.

Central to exploiting this skill is my belief in being a No.2! My AS means that interpersonal and political skills do not come naturally to me. Being loyal and supportive to someone, however, does. I enjoy working with people and being a sounding board; acting as a support mechanism and encouraging someone else are high motivators. These assets make me a hugely effective deputy. My talents in this field have been highly sought after by managers and have enabled me to reach high levels, ones that I perhaps could not have reached had I tried to assume the No.1 slot. Seniority is relative. Being second-in-command in a large organisation is more likely to confer greater responsibility than being No.1 in a small organisation. For a manager with AS, this has delivered huge benefits. I am less exposed to corporate politics; I am less likely to have to take decisions that impact negatively on others; and combined these reduce my levels of anxiety.

For many managers, managing staff is one of the hardest tasks. On the surface, for a manager with AS, this is potentially an even more problematic area, one that can be fraught with difficulties due to issues such as the poorer ability to empathise and communication barriers. Undoubtedly I have experienced difficulties in this area as a manager with AS. However, experience has contributed greatly towards realising significant improvement and my condition has afforded me real advantages when dealing with, and managing, people.

First of all is, as previously mentioned, my honesty and integrity. Most people know that they can trust and confide in me. However, there is also another important facet.

My logical mode of thinking means that I look at people rationally – and usually without prejudice or emotion. I am a fair person and do not allow personal feelings to impact negatively or influence things such as appraisals, career development or potential issues of conflict. I deal with facts, not personalities, and act accordingly. People appreciate this, especially over time. Though I have experienced difficulty initially with many relationships, difficulties that to start with have been to a degree a result of my AS, these have not been enduring.

During my career as a manager, the vast majority of people have come to like me and respect my integrity, honesty and basic decency. I have also gained respect for my inability to hold grudges. I have been forced to go through investigative processes as part of a disciplinary procedure but, at the end, the staff involved have not held it against me. Over time this brings enormous benefits from staff. People feel secure and not threatened, able to say what they truly think without fear of being ridiculed or belittled. They certainly don't, I believe, ever feel that I would seek retribution if personally challenged.

Finally, I am loyal: loyal to my staff and to my company. Loyalty too brings enormous benefits. People are loyal to me, and companies, as far as can be reasonably expected in today's volatile business environment, have generally reciprocated that loyalty.

Another key benefit of my personality is my passion. As someone with AS I care about things. The well-being of my staff and the direction and future of my company, and likewise of my superior, matter to me. It stems partly from my honesty, integrity and sense of values.

My passion drives me to want to make a contribution.

I am not money orientated; achievement, purpose and making a contribution are what matter and are what drive me personally. In the right business context this is infectious. Being seen to care and be passionate is a great motivator; it also impresses superiors and aids my ongoing progression.

I look now for roles that capture these values and allow me to excel. During my five years with a major leisure organisation my values were instrumental in the successes and achievements I delivered. I cared about the company, what it stood for and what it sought to achieve, and it came out in my work.

If things and an organisation matter, I am persistent. In my current company my energy, determination and sense of purpose have driven me to secure major contracts. I don't give up. My AS impresses upon me the importance of succeeding. Sure, I get bonuses when I deliver, which are very welcome personally, but it's the thought of ensuring that the company is viable, and that the employees within it can continue, that is the key motivator.

Part of this comes down to my inner strength. I have faced many difficulties as a result of having AS and, at times, have suffered from low morale and motivation. Some experiences in the business world have hit me personally very hard. But, ultimately, I have always come back, done better and improved, and this is down to my sense of self-worth that my condition affords me.

A teacher who has AS told me that she believes this as well. Deep down she knows she will succeed because, ultimately, she is independent and, to a large degree, on her own.

Having an "inner world" means that, as someone with AS, I know my mind and what I am about. I know therefore that I will always pull through no matter what happens. Within myself, I will never be beaten.

And perhaps this is what drives the successes I have achieved in business. And perhaps it drives the likes of Bill Gates – if he really does have AS – as well. Undoubtedly he possesses unique insights and has used these to make a huge contribution. Maybe others could not, for they do not have the skills, mindset or personal drivers of the average manager.

Malcolm Johnson has worked in senior management positions within the film, TV and games industries for over 13 years. His career has given him real insight into the issues affecting someone with AS operating in management positions. His experience has enabled him to develop effective strategies to cope with the issues confronting a manager with AS and, also, achieve real success in a variety of business contexts. Malcolm possesses Bachelor degrees in Geography and Psychology and an MBA from Warwick University Business School in the United Kingdom.

www.aspergermanagement.com

CHAPTER 8

SUPER STRENGTHS

Sondra Williams

I have multiple challenges navigating the world, interacting with and responding to others; I struggle greatly just navigating any setting or situation, but my life is not just a textbook of challenges. I also hold many strengths, and when properly supported can express them in successful ways.

One of my strengths is my ability to focus to detail and words, although my own syntax is odd and not well developed. I do not allow my syntax to be a barrier for me to express myself. I type out my thinking and let it flow, and later can use many supporting systems to do my best to repair and fix the grammar.

This strength allows me to use my ability to prepare PowerPoint presentations and speak before audiences of various sizes on autism. This is one area of my life I feel some life success in the ability to be self-employed. I am able to set my work hours, days, and times; I can work around my life schedule in ways that are not as complex and overwhelming to me as a so-called real job of having to clock in each day. One of my other successes in this area of my life is that speaking before large crowds does not produce a sense of fear or anxiety in the sense typically developing people feel. I instead have a different sort of anxiety in my speaking events; mostly based off sensory overloads and the fear of not being able to get my verbal output to flow. For I know if the sensory world or the expectations change or are too hard it can shut down my ability to speak, and this is the fear that can produce anxiety to me.

So far, I accommodate this fear by doing many self-adaptations in my speaking events, such as pressing hard onto my papers to give my hands a place to be rooted and not to be flapping in front of people. I also read poetry as my way to get the words flowing. Poetry is like music, and so the flow of it relaxes me and gets my words and scripts flowing too. I usually body rock or sway to keep self-regulated and centered. And lastly, I use a podium so that my written words are close to my eyes, which then allows me to look up to the audience and appear to be giving them eye contact and being engaged with them. All tools I use to present.

Another strength I have is that I am able to observe children within a setting and be able to interpret the child in an advanced way. Being able to see what most others will overlook. This strength has allowed me great success in working with young children with autism. This ability is not like a psychic person who can read the mind, but is more like one who can interpret actions, words, and behavior in an advanced way. In part I feel this gift is due to my own diagnosis of autism spectrum. My ability to feel, see, hear, smell, and taste the world around me in a more hyper fashion allows me to have an advantage over those who are not on the spectrum, because their sensory world is not altered to a pervasive fashion.

Within this ability area I can also rapidly read if the child is consumed by one of these sensory inputs that are disrupting their ability to connect to their environment. Due to my own autism I feel I have developed an odd system of my own gesturing that is consistent within me but often a mystery to others. For example, I am aware that when feeling lost or frustrated in a setting I might begin to play in odd fashions with my ear lobes, trying to tuck them into the ear canal, or will begin pulling at my hair or gently hitting myself. All forms of gesturing, that verbal words can't express at the moment that my system is overloaded. I feel that many people on the spectrum also have this odd gesturing/nonverbal language present, but many lack reading them for what they are. I find myself able to pick up rapidly on this odd nonverbal dialect, if you will, of the children and can see the patterns to them. This therefore brings me to a place of being able to interpret this nonverbal gesturing to the child's team at school or family and how to begin to use this language to support the child.

One of my strengths that most people respect is the ability to stay in tune to the words of others and be able to respond to them. While my autistic presentation is evident, most are impressed with my ability to get out my thinking, emotions, and feelings onto paper. Although I too can express myself verbally if well supported in the environment, I do best if the environment is very structured and presents a pattern that I can understand. Since one of my interest areas is autism, it gives me an advantage because I can be respected when it comes to working within many "autism-related" groups with success.

One of those groups is the Ohio Autism Task Force, to which I was appointed by the Governor of Ohio to serve as a voting member. It was a challenge for me in the sense of timing, as often I was not able to interact or express my views in good timing, but the way in which I self-adapted was that I later emailed my responses and thoughts to the board itself. This was a functional tool for me and the board itself respected my views as a voting member. They did not treat me as if I were the broken one on the board, or treat me as if I were autistic in a fashion of just allowing me to be present; they saw me and treated me as an equal partner in it all. I also serve as a board member for the Autism Society of Ohio, working on legislative changes. Here again my autism is not seen as a barrier to their work but as a way to enhance it.

I have been taking adapted ballet lessons for around a year now and gave my first dance recital in 2010. When I began dance I was greatly challenged with anxiety and the lack of coordination in moving my arms and legs at the same time in a structured fashion. Although now after much practice, I can move both my arms and legs in brief coordinated fashion.

This new skill has been challenging and yet very self-rewarding for me. I see dance as poetry in movement. I am trying so very hard to tell myself that my dance is a movement script and my work is rote-rehearsed verbal scripts. Dance is, though, for me a new found strength, and I have worked hard to overcome the fear and anxiety of movement. While I am still unable to dance in a group or with others yet, I will in time be able to work towards that as a personal goal.

Lastly, another area of strength for me is art. I love to spend hours cutting out pictures from magazines and dissecting words, phrases, and such into fragmented parts to create collages. My collages are my most profound way of expressing how I see and feel about the world around me.

When I create a collage it may take hours to match it up to a central theme or idea, or express how I see the person I am creating the art for. Many of them reflect strong humanity and ethical issues, and many are expressed in strong metaphorical fashions. These are considered a gift since those with autism are perceived as not being able to understand metaphors and/or grasp abstract meaning.

So, while many want to see our challenges as being the only thing prevalent within us, I hope that some will begin to see the strengths too. Many of us, if we are correctly supported in our areas of interest and ability, can have a life that is also with many successes as well. This book, I hope, will help others to see the ability of individuals on the spectrum more so than just focusing on the challenges.

Sondra Williams, diagnosed with an autistic spectrum disorder, has been married for nearly 20 years; is a parent of four children diagnosed with Asperger syndrome; and is also a grandmother. Sondra is self-employed and uses her abilities to find ways of meaningful employment for herself. She is also the author of the book titled Reflections of Self *and a DVD titled* Define Me. *Sondra serves as a board member of the Autism Society of Ohio, and on the advisory board for OCALI. She is a Parent Advocate trainee through the LEND Program of Ohio State University.*

PART 3

RELATIONSHIPS

In this section, three contributors share how their unique forms of communicating assist them to form new and to retain existing relationships.

Relationships are complicated, emotional and unpredictable – all very challenging for persons with ASD. If we, the neurotypical, have less of a challenge when it comes to relationships, this leads me to believe that we may need to meet our ASD persons more than half way and learn different forms of communicating to help the relationship have a strong foundation.

In return you may uncover a unique and different type of relationship/friendship to that you may have with neurotypicals, where you will discover that you both have different and yet also mutual needs that can be met in the relationship.

- *Wendy Lawson* shatters our beliefs about friendship and Asperger syndrome with an enlightening story about how loyal, honest and trustworthy an Aspie can be, and how they can offer traits that neurotypicals can't.

- *Stephen Shore* divulges how, when others reach into his world, they are able to form a close bond and then are able to see the benefits of having Asperger in a relationship.

- *Deborah Lipsky* conveys to us how her relationships and communications with animals gave her insight into understanding human social interactions.

CHAPTER 9

FRIENDSHIPS – ASPIE STYLE

Dr Wendy Lawson

That's a finch, probably a chaffinch. I can tell because of his song and how he dips and rises up again in flight in a flowing but continuous way. I have a passion for birds. Sometimes some of my friends share in this passion, but sometimes they are not interested. Being friends with someone means we probably have lots in common, but not always.

In the distance the sun rises, a glowing amber colour just behind the trees in front of me. Spring, what a glorious time of year. Many birds, animals, fish and all other manner of living creatures are seeking a mate. Having a mate, whether in the form of a lifetime partner or a best friend, seems like a good idea. I mean, it must be, or so many of us wouldn't spend so much time trying to find one!

"James, stop that!" yells his mother. James is beating up on some other kid. The other kid is howling and creating a big fuss. James is pulled off him by two grownups and his mum spanks him in the process. Why is it OK for a mum to spank if she is cross but it's not OK for James? Life is full of mysteries. Friendship can be a bit of a mystery at times too. One moment we like our friend, and the next one we are fighting with them. Maybe we fight sometimes because we know we can? I'm not sure. I do know, however, that real friends forgive each other their shortcomings and accept they have differences about things. I am learning about this.

Emotions can be powerful. There are feelings that draw you to someone and encourage you to seek out their company. Then something happens and those feelings change and you don't want to be near that person. If both sets of feelings are happening, does it mean that one set of feelings is a lie? How can we have both? How can both be true?

I think it's because circumstances frequently change, and this causes changes in how we feel about people. One could argue that human beings are fickle and that their changing emotive attitudes are like the weather. So, you never know what direction the wind might blow from!

Well, yes, this is human nature and being human can be an exciting disposition. We can enjoy the journey of discovery that is called friendship. The idea is that friends will travel the journey of life with us and, no matter what, they will be supportive and share in the ups and downs that come our way. The other idea is that this will be mutual and I get to share with them in the same way as they share with me.

Take my friend Chris, for example. He is someone I can depend upon to help me when I need him. He also knows that I will help him if he needs me. The other day I was alone at home and I was on my own for a whole week. I'm not very good at being on my own when it comes to my needing to go out to shops or into town to do things. I'm pretty good at being on my own at home otherwise. In fact I like being on my own, because I get to choose the things I want to do, like working on my computer.

Chris came over and he used his car to drive me to town to do the shopping. He carried the basket for me too, which was good because it was heavy. When we got home Chris asked me if he could help out in any other way for me. I put the kettle on and we sat down together so I could think about his proposal. Whilst we were drinking our cups of coffee I made a list of things that Chris could help me with. Chris talked to me about the things that were happening in his life, and it felt good to be able to encourage him in his ventures. We found, during the process of our conversing, that we had lots in common with each other and felt the same way about lots of things. After Chris left I felt very good inside that he had come and we had been able to spend some time together. I know that sometimes I am inclined to forget that other people might need me to listen to them as well as have me talk to them about what's happening for me.

"Wendy, you are one of the only people I can trust this with," said Miriam, another friend of mine. Other people have told me this too. It seems that it can be difficult for many people to share in each other's lives without believing that what they share will be safe with that person. Being an Aspie I think has many advantages for me. Although I think that my personality is a contributing factor, my Aspiness tends to mean that I am loyal and trustworthy. I don't have a need to gossip or pry into the affairs of others. It actually never occurs to me to do so.

For neurotypicals (the non-auties and non-Aspies) it seems that "keeping up appearances" and gossiping about others is an enjoyable pastime. I don't understand this. I think it undermines the whole concept of friendship. Being an Aspie means I'm not interested in these pursuits, and this is definitely an advantage when it comes to being a true friend to my friends.

Sometimes my phone rings. "Hi, Wendy. Could you come over and help me wash the dog? I need someone to help me hold him," says Helen.

"Of course I can," I say. We make an arrangement of time and Helen agrees to drive over and pick me up in her car. I could get a train, but it means walking to the station and this would take too long. The dog must be washed that morning and it's quicker if I get a lift over.

"Even my family don't like to help me with this," Helen says as she rubs the dog shampoo into Rupert's woolly coat. It's true it isn't any easy job. Rupert is a great dog; he is friendly and playful. He wouldn't bite you. But he hates having a bath, and this means he tries to jump out of the tub all the time. He makes me laugh because he shakes the water off his coat and I get soaked!

Helen and I laugh together a lot whilst we try to keep Rupert still and get him washed… I love it. After Rupert is finished having his bath we dry him off and keep him in by the heater to make sure he is dry enough and he won't just go and roll in the dirt and get all wet and muddy again. Once he is dry we let him go outside. Helen makes us both a cup of tea.

"I've got some gluten-free cookies here I bought to share with you," she says. I smile. It's so nice to be thought of and actually be able to sit and have a biscuit with my cup of tea.

"That's what friends do," says Helen. "They try to make sure their friends have the things they need or like; like the right biscuits to go with their tea."

Helen is a good friend and she says that I am a good friend to her because I am dependable.

"What do you think?" Dave asks me for my opinion.

Dave says he knows I will give him an honest opinion. "Not like Pete, who will tell me what I want to hear," Dave says. Being an Aspie allows me to be honest. This isn't always seen as a good quality and, it seems, at times people don't want to hear the truth. I know that my idea of "truth" might not always agree with someone else's, so this could be seen as "relative" truth. However, I will be honest if someone asks me. My friends respect this Aspie quality. I might not always know when my opinion isn't called for or when my friends don't need me to be honest with them. So, I ask them if they want me to say or if they prefer me not to express my views. This way I can try to avoid upsetting them. I find it interesting though that they quite often prefer me to tell them.

"Thanks for hanging in there with me, Wendy. All the others left. It was just too uncomfortable for them, they didn't know what to say or do. But, you just stayed. I appreciate that," says Bob.

I think that my Aspie disposition means that at times I don't need to know what the right words are or even what the expectation is… I just am happy to be. In some situations when others might be uncomfortable I am able to stay when they need to go. This is an asset in my friendships. Maybe it's got to do with not being concerned about appearances or about social graces? I just don't feel the discomfort.

I'm not aware at times of the emotional climate, so I get to go places where others might not. For example, after Bob's wife got sick and died. Bob said that initially people sent cards of condolences but then many of his "friends" kept away. He said it was because they didn't know how to handle it or what to say. For me though, these thoughts or feelings were not a concern. I kept up doing the things that I usually did. I still called over to visit with Bob, as I had done before. If Bob needed time on his own I knew he would have told me. He didn't say he did, so that meant I was welcome.

Being quite literal at times has gotten me into trouble with some of my friends. I am a bit "black and white" in some things and it's difficult to accommodate a changing playing field. However, if the rules change or if views and opinions change, I'm pretty good at coping if things are explained to me. One day Robyn, whose friendship was important to me, sent me a letter. It was a surprise to get a letter from her telling me she had moved house and wouldn't be able to see me for ages. I wondered why she hadn't told me before. When I asked her, she said she hadn't wanted to upset me. Actually, I'd rather have things explained to me and be given time to adjust to something being different than just be told afterwards. It might not be very comfortable, but the friendship journey is a shared one and we need to ride out the storms together.

Being as Aspie means I have all the same desires and needs just like anyone else. I need mates too. As a friend to my friends, I am loyal, long-suffering, trustworthy and committed to their best interests. I will give my honest opinion (when asked for) and I will always "go that extra mile". As Aspies, I reckon we have qualities that many others don't have. Probably though, this isn't their fault, it's just the way they are made.

Friends: A Good Idea

I want to be a friend to you,
This is a good idea.
Will you be my friend too?
Will you, will you, will you?

I know I can be stubborn,
At times you can be too.
I want to have a friend like you,
Do you, do you, do you?

I will be loyal, trustworthy and true.
I will be single minded,
I will be there for you.
Will you be there too, too, too?

You be my friend, I'll be your friend.
We will learn it's true.
Let's take our time to discover…
Thank you, thank you, thank you.

Wendy having a drink with friends

Wendy Lawson BSS, BSW(Hons), GDip(PsychStud), GDip(Psych), PhD is an autistic adult. Being a partner, mum, grandmother and friend to so many occupies Wendy's time and gives her great joy and satisfaction. When it comes to the autism spectrum, Wendy prefers the word "diffability" to disorder and her research seeks to explore what being differently abled means in the world of neurodiversity.

CHAPTER 10

A DIFFERENT
ORDER OF BEING

Stephen Shore

My wife and I have another discussion *again* about the protocol for our visiting her friends. We come in together, and after exchanging pleasantries, having dinner, I get to leave – as long as I promise to return to bring her home some hours later. Some couples may consider this reviewing of social protocol as unnecessary and a bother. However, we look at it as a way of "checking in." We are grateful of our ability to *talk* about things such as the rules for "couple visit" instead of leaving both of us guessing what the other is thinking – and possibly being disappointed when we are wrong. Good relationships require frequent communication. For those of us on the autism spectrum, perhaps the call for good communication is even more important.

A JOURNEY TO BUILDING A RELATIONSHIP

After typical development as a toddler, I was struck with the "autism bomb" or regressive autism at 18 months. Because there was so little information about autism in the early 1960s, it took a year for my parents to find a suitable place for diagnosis. Labeled with strong autistic tendencies, atypical development, with childhood psychosis, the doctors and other professionals recommended institutionalization.

It was during that time my parents had to implement what we would today refer to as an *intensive home-based, early intervention program emphasizing music, movement, sensory integration, narration, and imitation.* My mother did most of the work. Although Dad was present, in those days it was the father's job to hunt saber-tooth tigers or mastodons, leaving his spouse to do the "mommy" things. Initially, as many will do with an infant or young toddler, my mother tried to get me to imitate her. However, that not working, my mother switched things around and started imitating me. Once she did that I became aware of her in my environment.

What my parents did most closely resembled the developmental cognitive or affective approaches of today, such as the Miller Method (Miller 2007), or developmental individual and relationship (DIR) approaches, often known as Floortime (Greenspan and Wieder 2009), or Relational Development Intervention (Gutstein 2009). Focusing on how the child with autism perceives and thinks about the world and using that information to develop a relationship is a common thread binding these approaches together.

It was only by reaching into my world that we were able to form a close bond and then start bringing me into the greater universe. The key implication is that a connection with the other person must be made before any good relationship can begin. For people with autism, as well as many others, that means going into their world. An example might be if a child is flapping, you may want to get right down on the floor with them and flap... until they recognize you.

Due to the work of my parents, my verbal communication started returning at age four and I began attending the school I was initially rejected from. Fortunately, like so many parents of today, they advocated on my behalf – and convinced the school to enroll me. Psychologically oriented, the school prohibited communication about the child's day between the teachers and parents. The management feared that a mere parental request about whether their child ate lunch that day had the deeper psychological meaning of "Was the school a better parent to my child than I am?" And certainly a mere teacher did not have the psychiatric background to handle such weighty questions. Fortunately, I had a good teacher who seemed to understand her students with autism. This was not a good way to promote good relations with the parents, and thankfully there is now much better communication between educators and parents.

In elementary school I was a social and academic catastrophe, in that I did not know how to interact with my classmates in ways they expected or understood. I was about a grade behind in math and reading, causing me to be genuinely surprised when promoted to the next grade. My classmates were interested in toys and sports, neither of which held my attention. Bullies were a constant threat as they are for 95 percent or more of children on the autism spectrum (Dubin 2007; Heinrichs 2003). I was happy just to make it home at the end of the day where I could play with my chemistry set, build things using Lego, listen to classical music, take apart electronic equipment, and wait for nighttime so I could use my telescope to study astronomy.

Because my interests were so different from my classmates, that made it hard to develop any meaningful relationships with them. However, middle school changed that to a great degree. Due to my interest in taking apart radios and other things involving electricity, I was enrolled in an electronics shop class. However, combined with the instructor noticing I finished the coursework in about a month and there were problems with bullies in class, he had me transferred to the school band. In the band I could finally employ my deep interest in music to engage with my classmates. Talking about the music, practicing parts together, etc. formed the basis of true friendships.

Since I was a small child I have always liked bicycles. However, a true passion for anything related to bicycles began to form in middle school and carries on today. Getting involved with bicycling clubs was a great way to share my interests and develop platonic relationships with others.

The implication is that the deep passions of people on the autism spectrum can be an excellent way to develop successful interactions with others that can bloom into relationships. Bicycle- and music-based friendships continued through high school as well. However, the challenge of developing an intimate relationship with another person remained as I entered into university life.

Entering university life was a kind of utopia. Gone were the bullies. Classmates are now much more interesting and seemed to focus on who you were – as opposed to how much you were like someone else. Heck, if I wanted to ride my bicycle at midnight, I could find someone just as strange as I was to enjoy the wheeled quiet and darkness with me.

Vanquished were the boring classes where I awaited the high D♭ to float from the speaker signifying the end of a period. Instructors were more helpful. It was neat living on my own with a roommate I knew from my grade school days. The days of higher education were long, and still continue, as I am now a professor of special education at Adelphi University.

Part of the college experience involves dating; which entails a lot of unwritten rules and nonverbal communication. Often I wanted to date, but I never could figure out how it was done. In particular, determining the line of demarcation between platonic and intimate relations was particularly vexing. Queries to trusted friends resulting in answers similar to "You just know when it happens" made me wonder if crossing this line was like catching a fish – because that's the answer I got from my uncle when I asked him how I could tell when one was on the line.

My first (non) dating experience occurred as an undergraduate student. After spending much time with a friendly woman a few years older than me, she announced a strong fondness for backrubs and hugs.

Being hyposensitive in the vestibular and proprioceptive senses, I tend towards *sensory seeking* activities. A sensory seeker child, for example, may spin in circles, crawl under mattresses, and seek hugs in an attempt to find their physical being within the environment. As a youngster one of my favorite activities was to ride my bicycle headlong into a snow bank to experience flight as I launched myself over the handlebars. Add to this my literal thinking; I thought I had "struck gold" where I now had a new found friend – who doubled as a kind of deep-pressure Temple Grandin "Squeeze Machine" (Grandin 2006, p.58)!

This lady clearly had other ideas. After a lot of talking and tears on her part, I realized that not only did she want to be my girlfriend, but thought she had been dating me for about a month. I beat a hasty retreat. This error made me realize that there was a lot more to communication and relationships with others beyond the written and spoken word. There was a whole other area of interaction to be explored called nonverbal communication.

There is a myth that people with autism lack an ability to comprehend nonverbal communication. In actuality, we can learn to understand this channel of interaction very well –

sometimes even better than persons not on the autism spectrum. The difference is that while non-autistic persons learn this type of communication by observation, those with autism may need direct instruction. For younger children and some adults this may mean a social skills class or series of workshops. When I discovered my need to learn nonverbal communication it was 1984, a full decade before Asperger syndrome became a recognized condition (American Psychiatric Association 2000, p.68).

Fascinated at this newly discovered channel of communication I spent hours in bookstores poring over books on body language and other means of nonverbal communication. As a result I amassed a large lexicon of nonverbal interaction data points and can analyze this type of interaction fairly well, though it can still be difficult to practice my knowledge in real time. However imperfect my real-time processing of nonverbal interaction may be, this knowledge continues to be very helpful in my communications with others and understanding the "Hidden Curriculum" (Myles, Trautman and Schelvan 2004) that is such an important part of socialization.

My final dating experience started as a graduate student in music education. Being in the United States for only 18 months, a classmate from China asked me if I would help her understand the English aspects of a music theory class. In return she offered assistance with the musical components of the course.

Time spent in checking each other's homework morphed into doing things socially, such as attending a Chinese New Year's party or having dinner at her apartment. One day, while walking on a beach, she suddenly hugged and kissed me followed by holding my hand. It was at that point that the drill I had developed kicked in. "If a woman hugs, kisses, and holds your hand all at about the same time, it means she wants to be your girlfriend. At this point one of three answers is appropriate: 'Yes,' 'No,' or 'Further investigation and analysis is indicated.'" It seemed to be a good thing to do then, and remains as such as we have just celebrated our 19th wedding anniversary.

As suggested at the beginning, the awareness of my having Asperger syndrome means that it is already understood that less "mindreading" between us as a couple is going to happen. Being of different cultures accentuates the need for good communication about our thoughts and feelings. Without our recognition for the need for good communication, our marriage would be much more difficult and perhaps not even have lasted. It is my sense that the assumption that couples should be able to "mindread" each other's thoughts and feelings may cause many misunderstandings.

Like with any other couple, there will be misunderstandings and arguments. When they do occur we work to resolve them as quickly and fairly as possible.

THE INTERPLAY BETWEEN DIFFERENT CULTURES AND ASPERGER SYNDROME

I think there is also a specific way that culture can interplay positively for people on the autism spectrum seeking intimate relationships with others. All through grade school I was curious as to why almost all of my friends were older than me. Either I got along with my elder sister's friends or with adults. I was pleased to find my experiences validated when I read that children on the autism spectrum tend to get along better with adults than with peers of their own age (Attwood 2006).

As I entered the world of work after earning my bachelor degrees, I found that all of my friends hailed from other countries. And even now, I prefer people who are either older or younger than I am as well as those from other countries. My sense is that there is a three-part cultural explanation for this.

First, persons of another culture may not detect as many differences as another from one's own culture will. Persons from a given culture intimately know how another "should" behave in terms of nonverbal communications, phrasing, vocal prosody, clothing, and a number of other dimensions. This culturally based behavioral awareness may explain why people of certain minority groupings, such as expatriates and even people with autism, seem to have a sort of radar for finding similar people.

Second, persons from another culture may attribute behavioral variances to cultural differences. If the autism spectrum can be considered as a culture (Mesibov, Shea and Schopler 2004) then those noting these different actions are correct, although they may not be thinking specifically of autism as a culture.

Finally, it may be that because people of another culture are already content with integrating into a new society, there may be greater tolerances or even appreciation for differences. In part, this may be the reason my wife and I originally noticed each other, and have been married for almost two decades.

CONCLUSION

Understanding the characteristics of people on the autism spectrum and how they can be used as strengths for interacting with others will go far in developing successful relationships with those with autism. For example, instead of considering a "restricted interest" (American Psychiatric Association 2000) in trains as pathological and exclusive to developing relationships with others and learning, this fascination can be reframed as a "deep interest" (Paradiz 2002, p.140). Clubs and other organizations made up of people interested in trains could be found, just as my passion for bicycles opens a world of friendships with others also interested in bicycling. As for academics, the motivating power behind the affinity for trains can be used to teach mathematics, reading, social studies, and other topics. Later on, this intense interest could lead to relationships with friends and a significant other just as my passion led me to my wife, who came to study in the United States after nine years of serving as principal harpist of the Beijing Symphony in the People's Republic of China.

I have focused on relationships with others, primarily as a student and with my wife. However, there are many areas such as employment, getting along with others in the community, and others where developing positive interactions is vital to leading a fulfilling and productive life. The literature is rich with information about developing positive relationships in these areas.

In all, being on the autism spectrum does not have to be a disordered way of being...but rather a different order of being.

Stephen is a professor at Adelphi University in New York State where his research focuses on matching best practice to the needs of people with autism. In addition to working with children and talking about life on the autism spectrum, Stephen presents and consults internationally on adult issues pertinent to education, relationships, employment, advocacy and disclosure. Dr Shore serves in the Interagency Autism Coordinating Committee, and for the Board of Directors for Autism Society of America Unlocking Autism and other autism-related organisations.

REFERENCES

American Psychiatric Association (2000) *Diagnostic and Statistical Manual of Mental Disorders – Text Revision.* Washington, DC: American Psychiatric Association.

Attwood, A. (2006) *The Complete Guide to Asperger's Syndrome.* London: Jessica Kingsley Publishers.

Dubin, N. (2007) *Asperger Syndrome and Bullying: Strategies and Solutions.* London: Jessica Kingsley Publishers.

Grandin, T. (2006) *Thinking in Pictures, Expanded Edition: My Life with Autism.* New York: Vintage Books.

Greenspan, S. and Wieder, S. (2009) *Engaging Autism: Using the Floortime Approach to Help Children Relate, Communicate, and Think.* Cambridge, MA: Da Capo Lifelong Books.

Gutstein, S. (2009) *The RDI Book: Forging New Pathways for Autism, Asperger's, and PDD with the Relationships Development Intervention® Program.* Houston, TX: Connections Center.

Heinrichs, R. (2003) *Perfect Targets: Asperger Syndrome and Bullying – Practical Solutions for Surviving the Social World.* Shawnee Mission, KS: Autism Asperger Publishing Company.

Mesibov, G., Shea, V. and Schopler, E. (2004) *The TEACCH Approach to Autism Spectrum Disorders.* New York: Klewer Academic Press.

Miller, A. (2007) *The Miller Method®: Developing Capacities of Children on the Autism Spectrum.* London: Jessica Kingsley Publishers.

Myles, B., Trautman, M. and Schelvan, R. (2004) *The Hidden Curriculum: Practical Solutions for Understanding Unstated Rules in Social Situations.* Shawnee Mission, KS: Autism Asperger Publishing Company.

Paradiz, V. (2002) *Elijah's Cup: A Family's Journey into the Community and Culture of High-Functioning Autism and Asperger's Syndrome.* New York: The Free Press.

CHAPTER 11

TALKING TO
THE ANIMALS

Deborah Lipsky

Besides being an accomplished seminar and keynote presenter,
I am also known as the autistic comedian when I do speaking
engagements, and I have been told that my comedic timing and
interaction with people is outstanding. I am always asked how I
learned this skill proficiently, and people are amazed when I say
my greatest teachers are animals.

All my life I never could fit in with my peers or even humans,
but I had an uncanny ability to relate to and communicate

with animals even as a young child. I grew up in a time in American history where racial disdain for minorities was abundant. Scarcely 20 years had passed since Germany's defeat in 1945, and the area I lived in viewed all Germans as Nazis. Being German-born and raised, the daily physical assaults from my classmates commenced in first grade. My autistic behaviors, such as incessant rocking during class, my unwillingness to participate in group activities, my frequent meltdowns when school routines were interrupted by fire drills, substitute teachers, or being forced to stay after school for minor infractions – all of which led to my bolting out of the class and running out of the school countless times – did not put me in good graces with my teachers.

In the early and mid 1960s there was little understanding of the needs of children with intellectual/cognitive disabilities and certainly no diagnosis for high-functioning autistics like me. I was deemed a behavioral problem and sent to a "special ed" segregated classroom for children labeled at the time as "mentally retarded." As I was intellectually gifted the special ed teacher thankfully felt this setting was inappropriate and I was returned to regular classrooms after only a few weeks.

My only bright spot in the school day was lunch recess outdoors. While the other children played games, I would wander off to the meadow behind the school and watch the butterflies and bees flutter among the wild flowers. You see at home my mother would read to me from German children's books about elves and gnomes living in harmony in the forest with wild animals. The animals even took on human qualities as in the story of Puss in Boots. In the meadow by the school I would reflect on those stories and view myself as the same creature I was currently observing. There was an abundance of bumble bees with their bright-yellow large fuzzy bodies contrasted by black stripes among the flowers. Understanding they were collecting nectar, I would pick flower heads and dust my hands with pollen, then stash a daisy in my pocket. Gently I would approach a hovering bee and clasp it between my palms, allowing it to explore my fingers before watching it fly away. I would catch more than a dozen within the recess period. When the bell rang to signal our return to class, I would place a bumblebee in my pocket as my new friend.

As a six-year-old I was unable to adapt to the learning style of mainstream classrooms, so frequently during the school day I disengaged from the lesson at hand and retreated mentally to my world where animal creatures of all kinds lived harmoniously together. Reaching into my pocket I would fumble till I felt the bumblebee's buzzing, then ever so delicately pull it out with my fingers and place it on my hand. Time after time the bees seemed content to just wander up my arm or stay perched on top of my finger, flying away in panic only after failed swatting by an agitated teacher. For this I was always sent to sit in the class closet as punishment, but it did not deter me from catching more the next day. The remarkable thing you should know is after being stung for the first time by a bee as an adult it was evident I have a life-threatening allergy to bee stings. In the 1960s before epi-pens (epinephrine injections) were carried and used outside of a hospital setting by people allergic to bees, just one sting would have most likely resulted in my death, yet somehow I sensed the ability to relate and communicate to the bee in such a way neither one of us felt threatened by the other.

During lunch recess I frequently sat under the acorn tree in the schoolyard away from the other children that delighted in tormenting me. Gray squirrels were abundant among the grove of nut-bearing trees. As I sat I would mimic every note of the squirrel's incessant chatter as it stood on the limbs above me obviously infuriated that I was in its "territory." When the bell rang to summon us back to class I would always leave a part of my lunch behind as a "peace offering" for the squirrel.

It was only a matter of days before the squirrel would see me coming, scurry to the base of the tree where I normally sat, and begin to chirp in a non-threatened manner. I would sit down mimicking his chirps "verbatim" if you will. Whatever I "said," or perhaps it was the tone in which I spoke his language, intrigued him enough to meander up onto my knee and just quietly sit there observing me. Never making eye contact, I would slowly offer him a piece of my sandwich, which he gratefully took from my fingers. It didn't take him long to become so brave as to regularly scurry up my arm and perch himself on my shoulder for most of the recess period. I befriended many squirrels in various settings similar to this my entire childhood.

My love of animals continued into adulthood. I found a husband willing to move to the secluded woods of Northern Maine, and while he maintained a job outside of the farm I devoted my life to working with animals. I also became a licensed wildlife rehabilitator taking in injured and orphaned wild creatures. I specialized in small mammals, mainly skunks, raccoons, squirrels, fox, wild hares, and porcupines. My setting is idyllic for Northern Maine as it is a rural farming community. Aroostook County in which I live is the second leading potato producer in the country and still maintained by family farms. Huge wide-open potato fields mingle harmoniously with dense forested areas where wildlife and nature conservationists flourish. Aroostook County is at the very top of Maine, bordering Canada on three sides. We average 130 inches of snow every winter, and as a geographical area our county is the largest in Maine, comprising more than a quarter of the state.

It is still a place where you can safely ride a horse to town, violent crimes are shockingly rare, and deer herds grazing among the livestock are common sight. I own an 80-acre parcel of woodland and open fields overlooking Mount Katahdin (the tallest mountain in Maine), and my farm has 50 acres of pastures, fields, and landscaped woodland. It borders other large undeveloped acreage perfect for releasing wildlife back into the wild without the fear of them becoming a nuisance to neighbors. At night the stars shine vibrantly for there is no light pollution (excessive lights, street lamps, etc.). The entire county of Aroostook has approximately only 25,000 widely scattered human residents.

My social skills were so severely lacking that I had no desire to interact with the human world. My conversational social skills were limited to rambling monologues about my special interests, honest but tactless and poorly timed observations and comments, and frequent interrupting of others. Cloistered away on the farm I devoted my days to working with different livestock. I also specialized in caring and rehabilitating raccoons back into the wild. I learned so much about interactions with others by watching animal behavior among their kind that I applied that to my interactions with humans. I would need an entire book to cover all that I have learned, so here are just a few examples of the social skills I picked up from my four-footed friends.

I bond with horses rather quickly. Like so many other autistic people, my peripheral vision is highly advanced, just like animals that have eyes on the side of their head.

Like horses, I startle easy when I catch something out of the corner of my eye and my fight and flight responses are also heightened. As with horses, I didn't like people approaching me directly from the front or being touched without warning. I decided to "be myself" around them, and I would approach my horses from the side, never making direct eye contact, and always talking to them before touching. If you run up to a horse waving your arms squealing in delight – even if it is your horse – you will elicit a flight response and they bolt in the opposite direction. Only with women acquaintances (friends know better) do I encounter this, where if she recognizes me at a distance and hasn't seen me in awhile, I hear that screeching (like a banshee… of Celtic lore) and see that waving of arms, accompanied by a mad dash to run up to me to give me a hug. My first instinctual reaction is to flee like my hoofed counterparts, but I have learned not to. Instead I explain nicely that I have the same fight and flight tendencies as a horse caught off guard and approaching less demonstratively will avert that stunned look, the tensed-up and twitchy body positive that I display, or my appearing snobby by quickly running in the opposite direction.

I watched my horses exchange "friendship greetings" when new pasture mates were introduced, where they would put their heads over the shoulder of the other one and nibble their withers. First they would walk up to each other's muzzle and snort lightly into the other's nostril – sort of like saying "hello" in horse talk. This was relaxing and nonaggressive. Having observed this, I would talk to the horse in a low voice as I approached, placing my hand on their withers firmly (to mimic the weight of a horse's head), and begin to scratch that area.

It wasn't long after that all my equines would reciprocate and began to "scratch" my back as I scratched their withers. After this encounter the animals would be relaxed and open to further communication from me. Every animal species has some similar greeting, so I concluded this must also pertain to humans shaking hands when first meeting one another to show a non-threatening encounter. People use a smile instead of nostril blowing and say a short greeting like "Hello" or "Nice to meet you" and use this gesture first rather than starting right into a detailed conversation. The pasture greetings taught me to be relaxed in my body position, smile, say a short greeting phrase, and initiate this hand gesture in order to open a communication channel when meeting someone for the first time and waiting to see if they are receptive to further communication instead of launching right into a topic.

One of the greatest lessons I gained from my animal friends relates to death and grieving. It is a topic that human beings seem to be fearful of accepting as just the natural order of things in the universe. Mankind has even gone so far as to mask the finality of death with trite phrases such as "passed away," or "gone to be with the Lord," to make the inevitable seem more palatable. How to deal with a grieving person or even appropriate funeral behavior isn't readily found in books on social skills.

I had on impulse bought a Belgian draft horse I saw while at a livestock auction. Feeling like this animal had suffered so much in his life, I deliberately outbid the meat packing company for reasons that defied logic.

I saved him from the slaughterhouse. "Hercules" had been worked almost to death, evident by the malnutrition and horrific open sores known as shoulder galls from being forced to work for years in a harness too small. Chain marks were carved into his hide on his rear legs from iron chains attached to his harness. He was a broken down old man that didn't seem to care what his fate would be. When I got him home I tried in vain to revitalize him with good nutrition, new equine friends, and lots of brushing and petting. He failed to thrive. About a month later I bought a solid black Welsh cob pony named Sarah from a family that had outgrown her. When I introduced her to the herd, Hercules immediately bonded with her to the point they became inseparable. It was as if Sarah gave him the will and drive to live. Barely nine months had gone by and Hercules had put on all the weight he had lost and spent his days frolicking in the pasture with Sarah. Both his physical and emotional wounds were but a distant memory. It was quite comical to see this now massively built fully fleshed blond draft horse and Sarah, his little black "shadow," always beside him whether they were standing or walking. Both animals flourished and enjoyed this special friendship for three years.

One day I went out to pasture and I saw Sarah lying on the ground and Hercules standing over her. Immediately I sensed fear when Hercules whinnied to me as I approached. When I got her up and saw that she was suffering severe stomach pain I led her and Hercules to the barn and called the veterinarian. He diagnosed her with a minor case of colic, gave me some medicine, and said she would be fine. I will never forget as long as I live the expression in Sarah's eyes when I petted her forehead to reassure her she would be fine.

I knew instinctively from how she looked at me that she was telling me she was dying. The vet dismissed my concerns and left. I decided to keep her in the barn at first but she kept answering Hercules' now constant whinnying for her. I realized that if she were truly dying she would want to spend her remaining time with Hercules, so I let her out to pasture to be with him. The other horses (except Hercules) sensed something was wrong, so they kept their distance initially. I came back an hour later to find Sarah and Hercules nowhere in sight. My frantic search ended when I found the entire herd at the furthest end of the property. Sarah was on her knees, Hercules keeping vigil over her, and the remaining six horses had encircled her. Every time Sarah tried to get up the herd would whinny in encouragement. It was the most pitiful yet mystical sight to behold, because despite the belief that animals want to die alone Sarah wanted company. Her "herd mates" rallied around her. Tears began streaming down my face when Sarah tried to stand one last time but hadn't the strength. Trembling, she fell to her knees but refused to go down. In a single file each horse came up solemnly to her and nuzzled her nose for a moment then slowly uttered a low whinny as they walked past Hercules who still stood towering over her. After the last horse passed Sarah looked up at Hercules one last time and then collapsed to the ground and died. I witnessed all this from six feet away. I knelt on the ground sobbing uncontrollably. The other horses, on seeing me crumple to the ground in despair, came near to me. One at a time each horse approached me, lowered their head, sniffed my tears, and then nuzzled my face before walking away. All six horses followed this same routine. I understood that to be their gesture of condolences.

While I am still haunted by this painful memory, the interactions I witnessed that day have helped me react appropriately to someone who is grieving the loss of a loved one. Like my horses, when I am at a funeral I don't try to carry on a trivial conversation with the bereaved or guests. I offer a comforting hug (equivalent to a horse nuzzle as a sign of sympathy). Quietly I stay in the background, especially at wakes when people tend to gather in little groups and talk about everything but the deceased. I do not engage in such conversations, preferring to just offer my presence as a sign of solidarity and respect. Remembering the solemness of my horse's reactions to Sarah's final moments offers the perspective that it isn't necessary to offer the bereaved a flurry of verbal condolences that sometimes feel inappropriate or hollow such as "He lived a good life" or "Death isn't forever, you'll see him again one day."

This painful learning experience taught me that saying nothing and just being there is enough to convey your respect for the deceased and the bereaved.

I am particularly fond of cats. Cats mirror my autistic personality. Cats to me are autistic dogs. I share my house with eight feline companions. It is a natural bond I truly identify with and share, such as their need for routine, rituals, aloofness, etc. I jokingly tell my audiences that if I believed in reincarnation I was supposed to come back as a cat but somehow missed my mark and ended up human. Cats are hypervigilant all the time. When startled suddenly, their expression is identical whether it is due to a fly buzzing onto a windowpane or an axe murderer. Like many fellow autistic individuals, I am hypervigilant too.

When something extraneous shatters my immediate inner serenity, such as a fire alarm at a hotel or the sudden high-pitched squeals of delight from children at play, like "Mittens" I have the impulse to race away to a place of safety. Cats when "spooked" will run with incredible speed into the nearest nook and cranny managing to squeeze themselves into the tiniest of places. As a child, when suddenly startled just like cats, I too would head off for the nearest closet or under a table, or just someplace dark away from people, without forethought of personal safety. It is instinctual. As an adult I have learned to control this impulse most times, but having been around cats all my life I have learned that cats and autistic individuals share many similar traits, and it is part of who we are. This understanding is an invaluable social skills communication tool in helping me with my consultations with parents and professionals working with children on the autism spectrum to explain why there is a tendency blindly to bolt (run away) when frightened. It isn't the child trying to "manipulate" the situation, or doing it for attention.

Cats have also taught me a social skill on politeness. Since I love cats, I tend to spoil mine with treats on holidays and cat birthdays. I will go out of my way and buy a gourmet can of cat food with the anticipation of gratitude and purrs of delight from my kitties. With the fanfare equivalent to a human dinner party each cat gets their own special dish served to them individually. It never fails that at least one cat will, after sniffing this expensive feast, decide it is "fit for burial" and scratch imaginary cat litter with their paw over the plate. With indignation "Fluffy" will flick her tail and walk away in disgust.

Of course I am deeply disappointed by her lack of gratitude and preference for an inferior brand of dinner, but it has taught me an invaluable social skill. When at someone's house or gathering, even if the food is gourmet and not my usual bland diet, don't show obvious disgust and offend the hostess, or restaurant. I ask ahead of time what will be served or I read the menu before sitting down at higher-class eateries so that I don't end up acting like my cats and saying exactly what I think about the food.

Another social skill lesson came from rehabilitating a group of young raccoons by giving them whole fresh water clams to teach them how to open and eat this food source they would encounter back in the wild. Being very tactile, much like myself, they love to touch, fondle, and hold objects of interest. This of course peaks the curiosity of the other kits (youngsters) that now also want to handle that object of fascination. In this group play one baby would slowly approach the one with the clam and just watch for a while. Then slowly and non-threateningly they would extend their paw toward the object to "ask" if they could play with it. If the raccoon with the clam wanted to share, they backed off quietly and allowed the new one to gingerly pull it towards them and play for a while before extending their paw back as a gesture to let them know to return it. If another baby raccoon got all excited watching another play and then rushed up attempting to grab the clam away, it would result in screaming and a tug-of-war with fighting and biting quickly ensuing.

One of my special interests and passion is collecting WW2 militaria and I can spend hours alone engrossed in my passion. I didn't like anyone touching my "stuff," but the raccoon baby taught me that it was OK to let others who asked nicely handle my military collection. On many an occasion when company came to visit, some of them would notice my military collectibles displayed in each room. While I became busy preparing tea or coffee, it was very common for them to wander up impulsively to one of my helmets, undo the chinstrap without knowing how to do so properly, and take the helmet off the mannequin's head to examine it better, never once putting it back in the same way I had it displayed. I was concerned that rough handling would damage the fragile aging leather components of the headgear. My reaction was as instinctual as the raccoon, so I became vigilant with people who displayed an impulsive tendency just to grab an object without asking first by closing off access to certain rooms where I knew I wanted no touching, removing collectibles most likely to be handled before company arrived, and inviting the guests to help in the making and serving of refreshments, keeping their minds focused on the task at hand. Prior to the raccoon lesson I would get all upset under those circumstances and say something I would regret later.

When I observed people as they interacted with one another I quickly realized we as humans engage in social interactions and non-threatening reciprocal conversational patterns very similar to our animal counterparts. Over the last 20 years I have been able to convert countless lessons I learned regarding social interactions among animals to my encounters with people. It was, and is still, the best social-skills training program for myself. One main reason for this success is due to a trust issue.

As a young child unable to discern people's motives, especially my peers, I would believe everything they said because I couldn't separate fact from lies. Eventually it developed into mistrust and further isolation from social interactions. My salvation came from opening up to animals. Animals work on instinct and have no hidden agenda. Their body language mirrors what they are feeling at the moment. Wild creatures in particular are very distrustful of humans, a trait I truly had come to understand. Their lack of eye contact, preference for solitary pursuits, and heightened flight and fight response to sudden movement is exactly what I identified with. By "becoming" (non-autistic adults would call it "pretending to be") the same species of animal I wanted to communicate with, mimicking their behaviors to better understand their language, I gained their trust. I trusted them also, for I knew there was no hidden agenda within our interaction; we both lived only in the moment. By trusting animals as I grew up I became able to apply that trust to my relationships with humans.

Sharing my lunch as a way to show the squirrel I meant no harm and wanted to socialize with him taught me that having a friend over for dinner, going out to eat, or even meeting for coffee was a non-threatening, informal way of interacting with a person. Taking my cue from my furry friend, I allow the other person to initiate conversations to which I will respond in a manner they understand, as opposed to going on a tirade about my special interest. Even though I may be totally uninterested in the content, I understand that I must listen in order to be successful in this social setting.

Because people, unlike animals, aren't predictable, and some may make themselves appear what they are not, to this day I spend more than half of my time relating to animals. It helps maintain a balance that aids in my communication skills and encourages further human interactions. While each individual with autism has his or her own unique way of learning to adapt to society, for me, observing animal socialization behaviors acts as an important adjunct in my never-ending struggle to fit in socially in a world that I do not understand.

Deborah Lipsky MEd is a highly sought-after accomplished international presenter. Known as the "autistic comedian," her presentations on autism are both humorous and poignant. She is also the 2006 recipient of a Temple Grandin award and has co-authored a book on managing meltdowns.

www.autistic-raccoonlady.com

PART 4

CREATIVITY

As Dr Tony Attwood has stated, "With Asperger's, life is a stage. The curtain goes up while they are in public and down when they are at home."[1]

In this section, five contributors discuss how they use all types of artforms as vehicles to express themselves. Once they found an area within the arts that they could grasp, they focused on this area and used these creative methods to communicate.

And it is stated that persons with ASD have difficulty in communicating... Maybe we are just not listening?

- *Robert McLachlan* writes about how the skills he learnt through his life on stage with dance and musical theatre helped him develop his "character" and how he sometimes uses role-play with real social situations.

- *Donna Williams* claims that her autism built her relationship to musicality and this ultimately allowed her to find a bridge between her world and the external world.

- *Jeanette Purkis* illustrates her journey of self-discovery through her artwork, initially struggling to capture

---

1   Quote found at www.aspires-relationships.com/articles_relationships.htm (accessed 14 September 2011).

the essence of a person's facial features to becoming a successful artist specialising in Asperger reality.

- *Peter Myers* explains how his search for the definition of the "Outsider Artist" not only rang bells with his artwork, but as a person with Asperger.

- *Colin Webber* composes this contribution with the same passion that he composes his music with. He talks about the emotional journey through music and how he is an aural sculptor rather than a musician.

CHAPTER 12

LIFE ON STAGE

Robert McLachlan

As a young boy, I was encouraged to try different hobbies and interests. I tried things as diverse as horse riding, stamp collecting, square dancing, ballroom dancing, reading, singing and tennis, to name a few. Some of these I persevered with even to this day, others were only a brief phase. My family were keen square dancers when I was young. Several of my brothers were even square dance callers. As a young boy I was taken along to all the dances and would often be found asleep under people's chairs. One night when I was five, the dancers were a boy short; I was called up to fill the gap, and so began one of my more enduring hobbies – dancing. I continued to square dance for many years after this first try and I still dance (tap rather than square dancing) today.

Nothing appealed to me as strongly as when I tried performing. My first conscious memory of any sort of real performance was in the field of ballroom dancing. I was first sent along to ballroom classes when I was seven. I was very reluctant and had to be bribed to get there in the first place. Like all kids, I could be talked into almost anything at the prospect of a cool new toy. Of course, I was more focused on the reward I was getting than the activity I was sent to but, hey, at least I went and even participated. I blamed my sister for my enrolment in ballroom classes since she was already attending and my mother decided it would be "good" for me too. I guess being manipulated into going could have been a source of resentment later in my life, but it didn't turn out that way. I started to enjoy the challenge of learning ballroom, especially when I started working towards some practical exams. After a while, I was even teamed up with a partner and started entering competitions. Since I had already been square dancing for a couple of years, I didn't find the concept of dancing in close proximity to a girl that revolting. In fact, it just seemed like a pretty normal thing to do. I hadn't realised that as a young boy apparently I was supposed to be disgusted at being so close to girls!

Competition dancing really gave me something to focus on. Not only did I enjoy the physical aspect of dancing but there was also the challenge of trying to beat other couples. After a failure to win anything in our first few competitions, I started to get a little discouraged. At that point, I got a new partner. I have no recollection of why at this stage, but it may just have ensured my future participation in ballroom dancing. I remember my first competition with my new partner. I, the "old hand", was assuring my new partner after we danced that there was no chance of a prize and that it was pretty safe to go home. Imagine my surprise when our names were called out for a third place. So surprised in fact that I jumped and hit my head on the low ceiling of the counter I was sitting on. No permanent damage was sustained, fortunately, and I was still able to collect my prize. Suddenly, I was being congratulated on my performance and gradually I realised I could lose myself during competitions when I was performing (with my partner) for the crowd. This encouraged me to continue dancing. We continued to win prizes and I grew more attached to the performance aspects of dancing. Over the next 20 years, I changed partners several times but continued to compete and do examinations and to enjoy more and more the performance aspects of my dancing.

The first kind of performing I had the opportunity to try was competition ballroom dancing and examinations. This was so different to my "normal" life. Here I was encouraged to be different, to stand out from the crowd. Here I was allowed, even encouraged, to "show off" without the usual teasing and put-downs this behaviour engendered in my daily existence. I didn't have to try to be the same as everyone else. In fact, the whole idea was to be identifiable – to be the one to be noticed amongst many. In addition, since you were actually a boy doing dancing (ballroom dancing, no less!), it was expected that you would, in many ways, be odd. And an odd young fellow I was – at least by the standards of most of the kids I went to school with. I danced, for a start, a fact that seemed impossible to conceal from my schoolmates. I was very shy, socially inept, got reasonable grades, dressed in old-fashioned clothes and was hopeless at team games. I was considered a "goody goody". I had no idea whatsoever how to "fit in", how to be "cool" or popular, and I had some odd habits, like making strange noises and not sitting still.

I was extremely shy around strangers, almost to the point of being socially withdrawn. I was an introvert, who was forced to spend much time by myself because of non-acceptance by my peers. I had my own fantasy world. I would play elaborate games with my toys or lose myself in a book. At around age ten, I would sometimes (back in the days when it felt safe) wander off around the local neighbourhood for the day, exploring, adventuring and trying to keep a low profile. I enjoyed getting my hands dirty, and if I could find something to build, take apart or create, all the better. I came to prefer my own company to that of others since social interaction only seemed to bring me misery.

As I grew up, I learnt to be more and more unobtrusive. I learnt to blend in, to not stand out in a crowd, since this seemed a much safer course for me to take. Only one strange aspect of my life was an exception to this. How could this shy, introverted, unobtrusive person be out the front of stage dancing or performing? Looking back, it even seems strange to me. But I revelled in it. Performing allowed me to lose myself in the performance. I could be someone else for the duration of the performance, and in those days it was easier to be someone else than it was to be me. My problems and challenges would just seem to melt away as I felt the thrill and recognition of achieving and improving. It was my one chance to escape my frustrating, repressed life. So I grabbed the opportunities that arose with both hands. As I discovered the joy that the escape of performance could bring me, I threw myself deeply into it, despite the fact that, as a young boy, being a dancer just made me stand out from my peers even more. There was yet another good excuse for my peers to ostracise me. I was different from them in so many ways. Not only in who I was and how I behaved, but also in what I did in my spare time.

From the day I stepped out on the dance floor for my first real competition, I remember the thrill of performing. It was like putting aside who and what I usually was and taking on a "performance" persona. Taking on the characteristics that seemed to be needed for this particular performance was both a challenge and an escape. Ever since, I have spent much of my free time performing in one form or another. This took the form solely of dancing initially, but then I discovered the stage. Wow! This was a place designed specifically for one to lose one's "self" and become, at least temporarily, whomever the playwright has created. For a person who has had to struggle to learn and adopt many of the characteristics "normal" people have, this was a chance to put that skill into practice. It was taking a character, perhaps "normal", perhaps otherwise, and taking on those characteristics for a performance. It was putting on a social facade. This is what I was doing in my real life. The difference was, on stage, it was considered normal and was even worthy of praise and acclamation.

I often feel like I am playing a character in my own life. I have enough life experience and I am observant enough to know, in many situations, what is expected of me. On occasion, to make my own life easier or, at other times, to be considerate toward others I care about, I often play the character in my own life that is expected of me. This is sometimes a conscious decision and at other times becomes almost an automatic response to certain situations. Sometimes, it just seems like too much effort to do the "expected" thing, and people react by saying I am distant, remote or just that my behaviour is "out of character". Which of course it is. It is "out of (the) character" that I usually choose to play. Stage and dance performance has given me a wonderful tool to assist me in more easily integrating myself into society. It has allowed me to interact with people more easily and has been a guide to some of the mysteries that relationships present to me. Because of the contribution performance has made to my everyday existence, I am sure I will always have a fondness, if not a great love, of performing.

My full-time career is a job in the public service. While this has served me well as a secure, forgiving and comfortable way to earn a living, it is often uninspiring, bland and stifling. Dance and performance have been a wonderful release from the conformity of my everyday job and while I haven't always balanced work and hobbies well in my life, they *can* be balanced. Well, to go back to my alternative career on the stage – at certain stages in my life I have thrown myself wholeheartedly into the theatre. I have acted/sung/danced in as many as nine musicals/plays in one year. If you have any idea of the commitment involved in participating in one production, you will realise just what a massive effort nine involves and how it can basically become your whole life. This is not healthy of course. While one production a year is fun and a great showcase for my characterisations, it initially surprised me to learn that it didn't necessarily follow that nine productions would be even better. It became too hard to separate my life on stage from *my real life* and one production from the next one. As my skill in theatre performance grew, I wanted to do more and to challenge myself further. My inability to recognise when this became obsessive led to a stressful, unenjoyable experience that undermined my self-confidence and led to social withdrawal. As my ability on stage grew, my services were more in demand and I was still unable to see any reason to decline any opportunity to perform. I couldn't step back enough to see I was headed full steam ahead for a steep curve. I did get derailed, but fortunately only temporarily.

An occasional foray onto the stage though is a wonderful outlet and gives me a real sense of accomplishment. It gives me recognition for a talent that I developed, basically to make living my life easier. In that role, my acting talents remain hidden – no one realises I am doing anything out of the ordinary – which is a tribute to my skill in this area itself. So it is very nice to be able to apply my acting talents occasionally on stage and have them recognised for what they are.

Of course, being accomplished on stage brought offers for me to help out behind the scenes. I dance well, so why not choreograph a production; and I act well, so why not direct a production? It all sounded good in theory and I persevered with both of these opportunities for a number of years. However, I came to the realisation (slowly, I admit) that these activities were not giving me the opportunity to use my talent on stage where I could shine but were just forcing me into more social interactions where my characterisations are hidden and unacclaimed. True, they presented me with unique challenges and it is good to extend one's self, but it didn't provide the outlet for my uniqueness that dance and stage performances did.

For this reason, I have gradually moved away from these more complex involvements behind the scenes and have limited my theatrical activities to being on stage.

Dancing has become one of my great loves and accomplishments. When I dance, I can become somehow greater than my everyday self. I dance for my own enjoyment. If that involves a public performance, it entails the added thrill of performing and characterising for an audience. However, even if the audience is only myself, it still releases me from the usual social constraints, which I have become all too aware of over the course of my life. When I dance, I can forget about social expectations and behaviours and just concentrate on and even, on some exhilarating occasions, lose myself in the dance. On those special occasions when you feel yourself become the dance, it is like you have wings that have somehow been hidden and restrained your whole life and that are suddenly released, and you discover you can soar. This feeling might only last a few minutes but makes all the pain and frustration worthwhile.

At this stage, I find myself asking the question "Has my devotion to dance and theatre helped me in my normal, everyday existence?" I think the opportunity to soar when I dance and to characterise and escape my everyday character in the theatre gives me a release I wouldn't otherwise have. It allows me to plug away at my everyday existence with less resentment because that release is available. It allows me a glimpse of other lives and other ways to live.

Also, practising characterisations for the theatre and honing my acting skills to take on different roles has, I believe, helped me characterise and take on roles in my everyday life. While I still need lots of practice and I sometimes, despite myself, get out of character, dance and theatre has helped me take on a more acceptable, mainstream role and integrate more closely with a society in which I've always felt like an outsider.

Robert was born in Brisbane in 1963, the youngest of a family of seven. His parents were relatively older when he was born, his father was 47 and his mother was 40. He started dancing when he was five and performing when about 12. He was bullied unmercifully throughout his school years, and looking back he feels he was a very odd child and had a very unusual childhood. It took him a long time to realise he experienced the world differently to many others. He had no idea about Asperger syndrome until he met Josie and remains officially undiagnosed.

CHAPTER 13

DONNA WILLIAMS AND THE ASPINAUTS

Donna Williams

I grew up in a household full of music and the TV and radio blasting out jingles. I remember when I was three and a neighbour had commented on my singing (I had a vast repertoire of songs and jingles). I stopped singing due to exposure anxiety, which is not the same as shyness, nothing to do with it actually. I couldn't stand knowing I existed or anything trying to connect with me through my physical existence or expression. By age 9–11 I was left a record player and pile of old 78s. After exploring how the record player could be used to draw spirals on for the purpose of self-hypnosis, I began to play the records and became Louis Armstrong, Mitzi Gaynor, Bing Crosby and Ella Fitzgerald. But I was like Michigan J. Frog on the *Bugs Bunny Show*, as soon as I felt anyone watching me, exposure anxiety would grab my throat and choke my singing.

Nevertheless, by 19 I had begun song writing on the piano and by 22 had several songs and classical pieces. Finally I met a pianist and singer and allowed him to play and sing my songs. I was in love with the music and hearing it this way.

Then blasphemy, I passed the little piano room off the student cafeteria and to my horror heard my songs. I pulled open the door to find him performing them to a group of his friends. I took the music and left.

It was in my thirties, now living in the UK, that I dared to record my first album, *Nobody Nowhere* (same name as the book which was derived from the name of one of my poems which had become a song). I was terrified, knowing I couldn't sing with anyone directly watching. But I found a diversity-friendly producer, a producer of TV and film music, named Paul Farrer. I explained my issues and had a singer's booth so exposure anxiety let me sing, and this time in my own voice.

The album went up for sale in a local record shop, and then it went onto a site that sells works by independent artists, called CD Baby. Then my publisher began selling it. I was a singer-songwriter now with a selling album. I got an email from a Japanese TV director. He had bought the album, fallen in love with it and wanted two songs for his TV mini series *Things You Taught Me*. Its lead character was a woman with autism. Would I sell the rights? I agreed, and in the next year I travelled to Japan and met some of the cast and received the soundtrack album from the show featuring my songs. The sale paid for the production of the CD.

A few years passed and I moved back to Australia. Soon I took my many new songs to an Australian music producer, Akash. He was a man with Asperger's who is an accomplished musician and producer and helped run a Melbourne nightclub event for people with disabilities called Club Wild. Soon we had my second album, *Mutation*. The title track, "Beautiful Behavioural Mutations", went onto YouTube and had 20,000 hits in a year.

It was 2008 when Earl Wolff, a 60-something-year-old Aspie bass player from our local autism-friendly dinner club (started through Auties.org), kept nagging me to form a band. I knew a singer with autism, Belinda Mahoney, and resolved to team them up. Because I had already run a writers' group (which spawned Jeanette Purkis' book *Another Kind of Normal*) I set up a Melbourne artists' group with a view to mirroring the successful Autism Arts Expo already run in Adelaide by Katherine Annear.

I was in a cafe with Earl and a few others, but no Belinda. Finally, Earl looked at me and I conceded, OK, I'd be his singer. But we didn't have a guitarist, a drummer, or a keyboard player... Then young 20-something Andrew Bayliss walked in. I joked, "You wouldn't happen to play guitar, would you?" He did.

As we mused about the name of the band, I recalled a conversation with a young woman who was somewhere between autistic and Aspie. I'd resolved that she was "an Aspinaut". We'd chuckled. I suggested that as I was diagnosed with autism and Earl and Andrew were diagnosed with Asperger's, that we should be Donna and The Aspinauts.

Soon, I was at an autism conference as a public speaker. My rather Aspie husband Chris was chatting with a couple. The 30-something husband, Russell, was a keyboard player. He joined The Aspinauts. Next came a drummer we found on a muso website. It was awful. His banter and ego left us all feeling odd. We just had no idea what to do with it. Luckily, we weren't his "thing". Next came another drummer, a guy who was intense and speedy and utterly in his own world for reasons other than autism. We decided he fitted in.

But our new drummer, try as he did with all his passion, didn't yet have the dexterity or timing to keep tempo with the rest of us. Enter 20-something Andrew Sherman. There was something amazing from the moment he walked in. He muttered "hello", barely looking at us, took out his guitar and began to play like a pro. We waited another four rehearsals for him to converse with us, but that didn't really seem in his repertoire. It'd be a few more months before he'd really share much of who he was, and we determined this guy was on the spectrum.

As band manager, I wrote all the promo, set up our websites, and got us our first gigs. No pay, just door money and barely enough to cover petrol. I was terrified but the guys were thrilled. Then, a week before our first gig, our drummer pulled out. We were gutted. A friend of mine knew a drummer, Paul Spears, and put me in touch.

On meeting Paul I knew this guy was diversity-friendly. He just saw people not labels, he saw souls.

I loved his drumming and enjoyed the move to rehearse at his studio, PV Studios. It was a fabulously grungy place, a "boy's house", full of wood and coffee mugs, and a patch of grass out the back. The studio was homey and the atmosphere began to rock.

Paul was already in a band, The Soul Surfers, and was only "helping us out", but I couldn't see us finding another drummer who fitted us better, nor did I want to. As a pro drummer who had just turned 50 (we now had an Aspinaut representing every decade), he had done the rounds of pubs and clubs for pocket money eons ago, and though he became fond of us he didn't fancy any high level of commitment lugging his drums from one side of Melbourne to the other for no pay. But stay with us he did, and the gigs were fab and fun. We played several pubs with diversity-friendly audiences and a communal rapport that was priceless.

The shows were wild and funny and surreal. I was dressed in fishnet gloves, beret and clothes somewhere between Goth and punk and delivered combinations of rock, blues, skat and madness mixed with avant-garde poetry done with gestural signing and characterisations. We played together with well-known band The Vagrants, whose guitarist, Steve Iorio, described us as "Talking Heads meets Rocky Horror", and people agreed. Soon, descriptions such as Laurie Anderson and Piaf would be added, and Earl noted my phrasing reminded him of French chanson. Andrew was the archetypal rock guitarist, Russell was a theatrical, moody keyboard player, Earl was our old rocker bass player and Paul was our 70s hippy drummer.

We did stuff that was political, challenging and completely surreal. It was Taoist and sociological and often just downright silly. Musically it was rhythmic, rich and diverse. Yet with all our diversity – we had something, we had a "package". We began to move up and out into theatre atmospheres, doing "revue" type shows, the height of which was at a wonderful Rocky Horror-style theatre venue called The Butterfly Club. Tickets were $20 each. Would anybody pay that to see us? I really had no idea. But they did. We had a lovely audience, had an awesome time, and the vibe in the band was evolving, we could feel a change of direction.

Then Paul, our drummer, had a seizure and was diagnosed with a large cavernoma in his brain, a benign but, in his case, very large tumour. He was now struggling with all of his commitments. Like watching a bird struggling to fly, I knew someone had to take some of the weight off. I told him to drop his involvement with The Aspinauts.

We were now drummerless, even though we continued to meet at Paul's and record our first album there, *Broken Biscuit*, but we were about to get shakier. The keyboard player had family commitments, and somewhere between that and a falling out we were now without a keyboard player. Enter 20-something Anthony Julian, an Aspie with Tourette's who had been one of our number one fans and together with our loyal Aspie door clerk, Stuart Moore, had helped man the door at our gigs. Anthony had a music theatre background and played piano at an intermediate level, but I convinced him that what he lacked in playing he made up for in character.

Then Andrew Sherman needed to leave us to go fly planes as an aviator. That was a loss of an excellent guitarist. Now it was just myself, Earl and Anthony. Enter a 40-something conga player who could also play some guitar. Rather ADHD and quite the wild child, we resolved our new member would fit in.

We had turned other corners, too. With the film of *Nobody Nowhere* looming up ahead, I had my writer's shoes on. I produced our first rock musical, *Footsteps of a Nobody*. The show was quite avant-garde with Shakespearean spoken word performed in between songs which took the story further and told of my journey with autism from infancy to my twenties. We were moving into theatres and we were going to be paid.

Our first *Footsteps* show was at the Carlton Courthouse, a real Victorian courthouse turned theatre. We had a full house. Paul's commitments decreased and he rejoined us. It was wonderful to have him back, and I was determined to keep the level of commitments low.

Suddenly, we had our first funded booking. A service for special needs in Wodonga, called Cooinda, was going to fly us up, all expenses paid, supply the instruments at the other end and pay us to perform *Footsteps of a Nobody* at Wodonga Civic Centre. Me, Paul, Earl, Anthony and the conga player couldn't believe it. We were going on tour.

We arrived at the house we'd share, on a fab holiday resort. Our incredible host met us and supplied us a van, and had also done the shopping for us!

We had a picnic on the porch and enjoyed the camaraderie. The show was great, 80 people came. After the show I took questions and all the Aspinauts mingled and met with audience members. My grade 6 teacher, Mr Ryan ("Mr Reynolds" from the book *Nobody Nowhere*), had travelled over an hour to see the show. We loved doing the show and sharing the house, even doing the dishes together and trying to share a single toilet. There were three bedrooms. I had my own room and gave Paul the other room to himself on account of him being both drummer and our technical manager, doing our entire PA so essentially doing double the work of the others. Earl, Anthony and the conga player shared a room and fart jokes.

Soon, I'd written a second rock musical, this time a Dr Seuss-style fantasy, called *Baloombawop*, about a world where abnormality itself is normal and a raging conformist, Dame Grumpty Doo-bee The Fourth, was determined to "normalise" everyone and everything. This time I played seven characters, complete with costume changes, in one hour. We were now going to schools and libraries and had our first funded shows. It was an adjustment for the band, especially as Paul and Earl were "old rockers", but they rose to the challenge and it was silly and fun. We decided to divide the identity of the band into Donna and The Aspinauts (the band), Aspinauts For Kids (kids shows) and Aspinauts Players (a theatre company).

At our second theatre show a producer was in the audience, Harry Paternoster. He joined us and helped promote the shows, giving me a sense of how further to market them and that we might one day tour them nationally. Then a friend in the US linked me up with an autism-friendly theatre in LA, The Missing Piece Theatre, and I was taking the shows to the US. I wouldn't be taking the band yet; I'd perform them with a piano accompanist, David Moscoe, who had an adult son with autism. I was also to perform with them at two autism conferences, one in Long Beach, and one in New Jersey. We were excited. I even bought a van knowing we'd start touring in 2010. Then whilst riding his bike on the motorway, Earl, our bass player, was mobbed by magpies. He was in hospital with a broken shoulder and broken hip. We needed a replacement bass player for our next show. Enter, 69-year-old Derrick Nuttall, a funny comedian and pro musician from four hours out of Melbourne. He joined us just in time for a *Footsteps* show at the Guild Theatre. But, then, we turned another corner.

I had grown up with primary immune deficiency so had struggled with infections for my first 26 years of fairly constant antibiotics. I'd become immune to them and landed in the lap of allergists and immunologists. They glued me together with dietary interventions and immune boosters, so that by my late thirties I had recovered from a white cell deficiency and had normal IgA levels for the first time. But in September 2009, about to head off for a lecture tour to the UK, I developed bronchitis. It was unusual for me because I'd been almost bug-free for eight great years. By November I was on antibiotic number five and was diagnosed with an IgA and IgG2 deficiency. I was officially grounded.

If I flew, I'd risk pneumonia or worse and catch more bugs on the plane, bugs I had no immune system to fight. I cancelled my US appearances. By December I had pneumonia anyway. A few specialists and more antibiotics later, I was allergic to the antibiotics, had developed post-drug reactions and was advised to avoid crowds or children. Autoimmune disorders flared and it was clear I was in trouble. I finished off the *Broken Biscuit* album with The Aspinauts and got it up on CD Baby and announced it to the world. Then tried to sleep my way to health.

The Aspinauts would continue. But now they'd be waiting for me as I waited for my body. With an upcoming appointment with an immunologist, up ahead was the possibility of more shows and albums, but now my job was to stay healthy enough to remain part of that.

What I have discovered is that my autism built my relationship to musicality and to music, and ultimately that allowed me to find a bridge between my world and the external world.

Donna Williams is an Australian-born adult with autism who was assessed as psychotic at the age of two, labelled disturbed in her teens, and diagnosed as autistic in her twenties. She went on to become a qualified teacher with an honours degree in Sociology and a degree in Linguistics. She is the author of two international best-selling autobiographies and has ten published books. As a screenwriter, she wrote the screenplay to her book Nobody Nowhere, *which is currently under option to become a Hollywood film. She is also a professional artist, singer-songwriter and published poet as well as a world-renowned public speaker on autism.*

www.aspinauts.com; www.donnawilliams.net

CHAPTER 14

PORTRAITS

LEARNING HONESTY IN ART

Jeanette Purkis

Photograph by Adis Hondo

When in my final year of school I saw a painting by Frida Kahlo and I knew that was what I wanted to do – become an artist and paint portraits full of dark emotion and personal tragedy. As I was 17, I hadn't experienced anything much in the way of personal tragedy, unless you counted the years of bullying I had endured at school, or the constant embarrassment I seemed to suffer. But I thought I could make art that conveyed some far more mature emotions than I actually knew.

I started to make self-portraits, and was amazed that not only did they not convey any sense of emotion of any kind, they also looked nothing whatsoever like me. I figured that this must be because I was only starting out as an artist and did not possess the necessary skills in drawing to produce portraits that represented myself as I looked.

Self-portrait as a child

I found myself enrolled in art school a couple of years later. I still believed that to be a great artist one had to be able to represent the human face as a recognisable likeness of the person being portrayed. I drew everyone I knew: my friends, my teachers, myself, but always with the same result – they all looked like a person 20 years older who might be somehow related to the actual sitter.

My friend Julie was a case in point. Julie was suave and sophisticated, as far as I was concerned: a 24-year-old member of my socialist group and partner of an artist friend. Whenever I met Julie and her boyfriend I felt a need to be accepted; and, to me, that meant performing well in artistic endeavours while around my friends. I must have drawn Julie 30 times, but the results varied from the bizarre to the laughable. One time, Julie (who had two sisters with heroin addiction problems) was mortally offended when my charcoal drawing of her seemed coincidentally to be a representation of a terminal drug addiction case. Julie's drawn self had big dark eyes, sunken cheeks and a pallid complexion, and looked nothing like her, but probably did look rather like one of her sisters.

Lee, another friend, a man with boundless patience and a gentle, accepting nature, looked more like some kind of South American dictator in my one and only portrait of him. My lecturers at art school usually enjoyed looking at my portraits and probably saw them as psychological investigations of the human condition. But I felt that my lack of ability to produce a likeness of any of my friends in portrait form merely confirmed that I was a substandard artist who would never be able to represent the human face accurately.

I started to make some self-portraits, thinking that I would be able to represent myself with some degree of recognisability, given that I saw my own face in the mirror every day. Unfortunately my attempts at self-portraiture were no less frustrating than my efforts to draw my friends. I was 19 years old, yet every drawing I made of myself looked like a scary, even psychotic, 45-year-old woman. Her eyes would glare out at viewers as they tried to understand why I drew and painted myself as this ogre. I'm sure viewers of these portraits thought I had major issues with my view of myself, that I had little self-esteem or that I had some dark secrets to hide away. I did not in fact have any of these issues. What I did have was Asperger syndrome.

All my life, the human face has been a source of puzzlement. I have always had difficulties recognising people that I've known for a short while, and even sometimes find close friends hard to place if they're not in their usual context. At age 19, the features of the face meant little to me and I blocked them out. I rarely looked at other people's faces when I spoke to them, preferring to gaze down at the ground, or around into the street or the room, and even people I did look at baffled me if they changed their hairstyle or started wearing glasses. When I sat down to paint a portrait, I had no way of knowing what to do. I didn't know what an individual nose looked like, or how the face was constructed. I was envious of artists who could capture the likeness of the human face, because it was something that had always eluded me. At the time I was making portraits I did not know I had Asperger syndrome, and therefore had no way of realising why I had such difficulties with faces. I surmised that I must be an inferior artist or that maybe I had a mental block on drawing the human face.

By the time I was diagnosed with Asperger syndrome, at age 20, I did not accept the diagnosis, preferring to be what I thought was "cool" (which to me at that time included using drugs, committing crimes and associating with dubious characters who had little appreciation of art and less understanding of difference and disability). I did continue to draw and paint self-portraits, but I interpreted the evil glare of my drawings' eyes as simply a representation of my inner angst and difficult relationship to the world and the people in it. I stopped wanting to be a great artist and started just to draw and paint through an innate necessity to create that my drug-addled self could not pin down or explain. I had creativity within me that nothing seemed able to escape, and I continued to see myself as an artist even while serving a prison sentence.

I escaped the world of crime and drugs and decided to re-enrol in art school. I associated gaining my degree with success and I had been drawing or painting for the past ten years, so figured I would have a good portfolio to show to the various art institutions. I had a positively enormous collection of self-portraits by this stage.

There were my early ones in which an old woman's eyes pierced the viewer with their evil gaze. There were the ones I had done in prison which, surprisingly, were a close likeness of myself. There were the ones I had done in psychiatric hospital, which were so frightening I had to keep them under the bed. There was one, a painting that looked like a ghost, which I had hung over my bed, until it gave me nightmares and I took it down and hid it with the ones from hospital. Of all these dozens of drawings, very few had any essence of me in them. Strangely, very few people had ever commented about this lack of likeness in my portraits when I was at art school as a teenager. They had told me they were "spooky" or "disturbing", but no one had told me they didn't look like me, and I had not been able to realise that myself. I had assumed that I looked like these pictures, yet, when I looked in the mirror, the face staring back at me was not the face of my self-portraits. I did not have the ability to distinguish between what I really looked like and what I thought I looked like.

I still figured that to be unable to paint my own portrait was a sign that I was not a good artist. It was, to me, a mark of my failure that my drawings of myself looked nothing like me, yet it actually represented a lack of faith in myself. The idea of being able to paint my portrait accurately was a non-Asperger one that I had imposed on myself. Non-autistic artists can often represent people with an essence of their personality, as can some autistic and Asperger artists, but I will never have the ability to portray another person with anything approaching a likeness as I do not have the facility to recognise and process the human face. My wish to represent others and myself accurately through portraiture can be seen as a wish to be something other than who I actually was.

Throughout my first year at my new art school I was still haunted by a wish to represent myself and felt my inability to do so marked my failure as an artist. But at the start of my second year something happened that changed the way I saw myself and my art for ever – I accepted that I had Asperger syndrome and, as a result, began to accept myself for who I was. I finally understood why portraits had always been so frustrating for me and understood that I would probably never be able to draw or paint a likeness of another person or myself. I started to make artworks dealing with things that were important to me and that represented issues I had an interest in. I made works that looked at suicide attempts, and then prison, then drug use, but they had a deadpan humour instilled in them, something that tied in with trends in contemporary art at the time. I started to look forward to going into my studio and making works about issues from my past and didn't even mind that I was exposing things about myself to my fellow students that I had never divulged before. I infused my works with ideas of difference and diversity and with my slightly unusual, "Aspergerish" perspective on life. In a way, I was making self-portraits, or at least representing myself through my art, but I was doing it in a way that was true to who I was and that I had no trouble accomplishing.

I started to use words in my paintings and found that the sentences and paragraphs I added to the works had an ironic wit that appealed to lecturers and students alike. After years of slogging away unsuccessfully at portraiture, I had discovered a way of making art that most people enjoyed looking at and, more importantly, was an honest and feasible way for me to explore my ideas as an artist. I started to show my work at galleries around Melbourne, where I lived, and had an artist review one of my exhibitions in a contemporary arts magazine. From being an art student that spent her time in the studio being frustrated and jealous of the other, more successful students, I had become a successful artist myself simply by being myself. My new artworks were almost effortless. I would have an idea for a project, then simply carry it out. There was no frustration at all; rather, making art was a joyful and almost liberating experience.

I am an Asperger mimic; that is, I like to take on the expectations and actions of other people around me. This may seem, to some, to be an advantage, as it means that I can get through life without people thinking I'm weird and I can work out what's expected of me from other people and fulfil their needs. A person with Asperger syndrome who is not a mimic may find that hard. Being a mimic, however, is a hard thing for the person that is living with it. My mimicry meant that I imposed the expectation of needing to paint portraits of myself, and was totally trapped as an artist by what I thought the wishes of others were; of all the expectations of others I placed on myself in my life, that was probably the least damaging.

When I broke free of the need to please others and fulfil what I believed their expectations of me were, I found myself as an artist for the first time. Being a true version of who I was, making art about things that mattered to me, rather than simply acting the part of an artist, meant that I could pour my passion into what I did and finally succeed.

I have learned to use my Asperger perspective, together with ideas of diversity that so many people with disabilities have to deal with, to create an art practice that others in the art world, and some beyond it, seem to find interesting and original. By accepting my Asperger syndrome and using it to my advantage, I have become a successful artist and helped to introduce others to Asperger reality.

Jeanette Purkis is in her early thirties and has Asperger syndrome. Jeanette lives in Canberra, Australia. She is the author of Finding a Different Kind of Normal: Misadventures with Asperger Syndrome, *an autobiography published by Jessica Kingsley Publishers. Jeanette has a Masters degree in art and currently works as a civil servant (which she feels is a perfect job for a person who loves order and protocol). Jeanette advises people on the autism spectrum to draw on their unique experiences and work towards achieving their dreams.*

CHAPTER 15

ASPERGER SYNDROME

HOW IT AND ART INFLUENCE ME

Peter Myers

The first creative act in relation to myself occurred before I existed, but without which I would not. So it was that I was conceived, in Africa, sometime around September 1958, and born some nine months later, in a "gilly" (sandstorm), in the Sahara desert, 1st June 1959, just in time for dinner.

I have no conscious memories of Libya, where I lived until 15 months old. There are photos of my christening, at All Saints Church, Tobruk, 1st July 1959. And for the vast sum of two pounds and ten shillings, I was made a subject of her Britannic Majesty, Betty. So for the first month of life, after birth, I assume I was free. I have two birth certificates, one signed by a Wing Commander.

The first photo of my doing something creative was playing on the beach in Tobruk with a bucket and spade, seemingly deep in thought, of what I cannot recall.

The Sahara Desert might seem an ideal place for play with sand, particularly on the coast. However, most deserts are mainly rock, as means my name, Peter. My middle name, Terence, means "smooth" or "polished", so may fit with "rock". My surname, Myers, means "dweller by the marsh". So a desert may be a mighty strange place for a descendant of swamp people to be. One is wet, the other dry, and a peat bog child may not usually be found here.

My family returned to England, and I visited it for the first time.

"Art Brut", or "Outsider Art", consists of works produced by people who for various reasons have not been culturally indoctrinated or socially conditioned. They are all kinds of dwellers on the fringes of society. Working outside the fine arts "system" (schools, galleries, museums and so on), these people have produced, from the depths of their own personalities and for themselves and no one else, works of outstanding originality in concept, subject and techniques. They are works which owe nothing to tradition or fashion.

A firm distinction should be made between "Art Brut" and what is known as "Naif Art". The naif or primitive painters remain within the mainstream of painting proper, even if they fail ingeniously to practice its style. However, they accept its subjects, techniques (generally oils) and even its values, because they hope for public, if not official, recognition. "Art Brut" artists, on the other hand, make up their own techniques, often with new means and materials. And they create their works for their own use, as a kind of private theatre. They choose subjects which are often enigmatic and they do not care about the good opinion of others, even keeping their work secret.

(Michel Thévoz, Curator of the Collection de L'Art Brut in Lausanne, in *Art Brut*, published by Booking International, New York, 1976)

I have Asperger syndrome. The awareness of this came somewhat late in life. I self-diagnosed in 1992, and through a desire to know the who and what that I am, sought and received a formal assessment and diagnosis of this in 1996. So while being fairly mature in years, I am simultaneously "a new kid on the block".

Art, a creative outlet, is intrinsic to my nature, for as far back as I can recall, and is essential for my well-being. So I was intrigued as to how autism might influence my art, as well as myself as a person. Each would seem related to the other, part of the whole that is Peter. This contribution comprises some of my thoughts about this, and why I may be considered an "Outsider Artist".

I was introduced to the concept of "Outsider Art" by an American chap called Greg Wallace (from Washington D.C.). He was conducting a study into Asperger syndrome (at the Institute of Psychiatry, London), and I had agreed to participate in this.

I had shown Greg examples of my artwork, and it was after this that he suggested I might be an "Outsider Artist". During the course of his work, he has encountered a number of individuals on the autistic spectrum who possess specific abilities and who might be termed autistic savants, and he suggested that I might be one myself.

My understanding of savants was that their level of global functioning is quite low, below average, sometimes extremely deficient. However, in perhaps one area only (an islet of ability), they may possess a skill, gift, that far exceeds the norm, and may allow them to do this one thing superbly well (e.g. musical skills, mathematical calculation, artistic talent, phenomenal memory feats), superior to others, or simply allow them to do what others cannot.

The trade-off seems to be "having all one's eggs in one basket". It is as if all their energies and ability are concentrated in this one area only, sacrificing or impeding all other areas of functioning. Or perhaps it is "the path of least resistance".

From my own experience, I know that I do not possess the same gross global deficits in functioning. I do experience the same triad of impairments, or differences, which Lorna Wing outlined from her work on autism/Asperger syndrome, that of social communication, social imagination, social interaction. Basically, anything with a high social content and I will be disadvantaged. So these I tend to avoid.

And I know enough to get by, fake it, fudge it, mimic it, plain guess, and I can survive, muddle through, somehow. What I may lack in social empathy, I may make up for by "trial and error", constructing rules to live by, function, to make it through another day. I have made thousands upon thousands of mistakes, and I shall make thousands upon thousands more, as "those who do not learn from their mistakes are doomed to repeat them". Although I am better than I was, by far.

I am not sure if wisdom does indeed come with age. Perhaps one simply gets older. There is a quotation, "When I was a child I thought I knew everything. Now that I am an adult I realise I know nothing." If one thinks one knows everything, paradoxically one's mind may be closed to anything. However, if one thinks one knows nothing, then one's mind may be open to everything. Perhaps this is the wisdom.

One may read books about cars (e.g. models, the highway code, how to build a car, how individual car parts work), yet it does not follow that this is the same as the actual experience of driving a car, knowing how to drive a car.

Being on the autistic spectrum may be like this, having to learn every little thing the hard way, as seemingly nothing comes naturally, instinctively, intuitively – all the things others seem to take for granted, do not seem to have to think about, find easy. However, my difficulties seem minimal in comparison to many others on the spectrum. Yet I am on the autistic spectrum, and throughout my life, and in comparison to non-autistic others, all I sense are differences.

It is like having no sense of belonging, not fitting in, being a perpetual outsider, an alien on one's own planet, or, as Donna Williams outlined in a poem in her first book, like a "Nobody Nowhere". It is a sense many autistics may share.

Thinking about what Greg had suggested, about my being a savant, I stated my doubts to him about this, about my high level of functioning and more global abilities nullifying this. However, on the basis of meeting me, my participation in psychological tests, and viewing my artwork, he still considered this may be so.

So as I was intrigued by this term "Outsider Art", I decided to explore it further. I could not find much in the way of books on this subject, and what I did find did not seem to explain much – illustrate yes, but I could discern no coherent pattern as such.

My computer skills are minimal, and I may describe myself as "computer illiterate". Some who see my artwork may assume that I use a computer to create my pictures. This is not so. I would not know how. Instead, I draw the old-fashioned way, that of hand, eye, brain.

However, on a good day, and if someone provides a computer, and sets it up for me, I can access the internet, and have found this to be a very fast, efficient way of obtaining information. One of the best sites on the world wide web for "Outsider Art" that I have discovered is the Henry Boxer Gallery (www.outsiderart.co.uk). It also includes information on "Naive Self-taught Artists" and "Visionary Artists", as well as on specific artists, such as Stephen Wiltshire and Charles Bronson, whose work I shall explore further, as well as to make comparisons with my own.

"Naive Self-taught Artists" seem similar to "Outsider Artists" and "Visionary Artists", as well as professional artists themselves. They differ from professional artists (who may have been trained via college and academic qualifications) in that they are self-taught, and have avoided this process of social conditioning, leaving their art more "naive", less influenced by others or formal training.

Their subject matter is relatively conventional, comprising realistic scenes, minute detail, people, animals, the world, fantasy. However, they may desire official recognition and equal status with the professional artist, perhaps with a desire to become part of the art establishment itself.

Listed on the Henry Boxer website, under "Naive Self-taught Artists", is Stephen Wiltshire. I know a little of Stephen Wiltshire. He is at a different end of the autistic spectrum to myself, and may, I feel, be classed as an autistic savant, in the very real sense of the word. He possesses a remarkable talent for perspective, visual memory (perhaps photographic memory), and the ability to draw in almost perfect detail what he has once seen. This I cannot do, so I do something else.

He is, I think, the most well-known and respected of autistic artists, and artistic ability in autism is somewhat rare. I know of some: a boy in Japan who draws insects, Nadia in the UK who drew horses, Barbara Moran in the USA who draws traffic light and church figures, and Jessy Park in the USA who draws wonderfully colourful buildings, bridges, interiors.

I like patterns, detail, and things of interest to me.

Temple Grandin, a lady with high-functioning autism, has suggested that "non-autistics move from the general to the specific, whereas autistics move from the specific to the general". So here is a very real difference between the two.

My way of drawing is a little like this. I tend to concentrate on specific detail, as opposed to the composition as a whole.

Stephen is noted for his architectural drawings, in pencil, and in ink. However, his art progresses, and he now works in colour also, and his subject matter is widening, particularly since his visit to the USA and other parts of the world, and includes American cars, street scenes.

Viewing the website, I was surprised to see him listed as a "Naive Self-taught Artist", as due to his autism I thought he might come under the auspices of "Outsider Artist", but this may be due in part to his subject matter, that of architectural perspectives.

"Visionary Artists" seem to be exactly that, in that their work seems visionary, fantastical, mystical perhaps.

I like the term "Outsider Artist", as described by the Henry Boxer website. It would seem to fit not only myself as an artist, but also as a person.

If one sought an individual who had not been culturally indoctrinated or socially conditioned, then a hermit, an alien, or someone on the autistic spectrum might suit. It sort of "goes with the territory", and may confer such a person with a fairly unique perspective.

It is like being in a society, but not truly a part of it. An autistic person could go through college training, but still come out the other side, relatively untouched, or at least with their own individual perception intact. They may learn many things, yet persist in doing things in their own way, not a taught way, but in a way indicative of themselves.

I did art at school, was taught by the same teachers, used the same materials as other children, but have still developed a style I feel is uniquely my own.

When I was younger, particularly as a child, when I did a drawing, this was primarily for myself. Anxiety would preclude my sharing a picture with others. Indeed, anyone looking at my pictures might be the last thing I would desire.

For myself, art, drawing, was a very personal thing, a direct connection to my inner being, self to self (conscious to subconscious, and vice versa).

If I did art that was the same as others, I would think, "What is the point?" For myself I wish to do something different, unique, individual, of me. Art is a creative process. Simply to copy would seem to nullify this process, and I would rapidly lose interest.

Some of my work may seem repetitive (developing a theme, pattern, idea); however, they all differ from each other and show continual development, while keeping to my particular style. When I get bored, or have done an idea to death, I may move on, try something different.

If one does something for self, then being "mainstream" is largely an irrelevance.

I can draw traditional art subjects if requested (e.g. school, college, work). However, landscapes, seascapes, portraits, animals do not really interest me that much.

Many professional artists may be inspired by the world, and the things within it, however they may interpret this.

I tend to "see what I draw", as opposed to "draw what I see". I do not see a picture "in my mind's eye" and draw that (I do see such images, but they move too fast, constantly shifting, changing). Instead I tend to sense, feel, what it is that I wish to draw, and draw that, then I can see it.

My style of drawing is as much a subconscious as it is a conscious process. So my subject matter is not the world, but an inner world, and by the process of drawing is expressed outwardly.

I may be shown how to do something, but there remains within me a desire to do something my own way, put my mark upon it, make it my own, unique.

The Henry Boxer website cites Charles Bronson as an "Outsider Artist". This I found most interesting, as being dubbed "the most dangerous man currently incarcerated at Her Majesty's pleasure", and being in prison for so long (the majority of his adult life), he seems more of an "Insider Artist".

In a sense, I would perceive him as a "Naive Self-taught Artist". And indeed through growing recognition of his work, this might be considered so.

Indeed, it may raise the paradox of, once discovered and commercialised, can one continue to be an "Outsider Artist", even if one is inside? Charles Bronson's work may seem disturbing, fascinating, yet honest. It has a naivety about it, and wit.

His art may be a form of self-therapy, a mode of expression, chronicling a life, his life.

Although my own work is quite different, I can recognise the childlike nature of this work, not as a mark of disrespect, but as an observation of the frightened child within the man.

I am reminded of drawings I did at school, in an environment that had me in a constant state of high anxiety, stress, fear. Indeed, I feel the worst aspect of school was that it was full of other children.

My drawings of that time were characteristic of those I have seen of children who experience manic-depressive illness. Although I tend to be more hypo than hyper in nature. I do have a tendency towards depression when under stress, and school was a high-stress environment.

Dr Tony Attwood has said that in over 22 years of clinical experience, he has yet to meet a person with Asperger syndrome who was not traumatised by their experience of school. I would tend to agree, and add, similar to horrific experience in times of war, that such children may develop a form of post-traumatic shock from their experiences. I know I did.

Such experience may take years, decades, a lifetime to recover from, and/or that experience may stay with a person for life, reliving the past in the present.

There are good schools and bad ones, good teachers and bad ones. And children may be "little angels", or simply "children", or incredibly cruel and malicious.

Society, I feel, has an obligation to care for its most vulnerable members, and children, particularly autistic children, may be some of those at greatest risk. If a society does not care, then traumatised children may become mentally scarred adults, and that cannot be a good thing for a society, can it?

Drawing is a thing I have done, used throughout life, sometimes as a self-induced therapy, working things out with self. So I can appreciate why Mr Bronson might do likewise.

There is an optical, illusionary, almost hypnotic quality to some of my work. In some of my other work (particularly work in colour), I have occasionally been asked "If I look long enough will I see anything emerge?" which I think is a confusion with the "magical eye", 3D computer-generated art. So I reassure people, "No you will only get a headache."

Autistics tend to have superior ability in the "embedded figure test", that is discerning shapes, patterns, hidden within surrounding detail, and this seems to be innate. My own drawing may reflect that.

Children possess an ability to visualise which is superior to adults', something that is lost, diminished over time, as their capacity for language and other learning proceeds. Perhaps swapping one skill for another, learning one skill, forgetting another.

I do not feel that I consciously attempt to emulate the work of other artists, yet the subconscious is such a mischievous thing, and even autistics may be influenced by the world around them, to a greater or lesser extent, if only in the medium that is available to them.

Backgrounds may differ, yet artists may touch upon similar territory, albeit by different routes, and with diverging aims, objectives, in mind.

I do feel that there are certain patterns embedded within the human psyche, and that they are innate in everyone, and accessible to those who know how. Thus similar patterns may be found in ancient European art, Celtic art, cave paintings, North American art, South American art, Central American art, Aboriginal art, African art, Islamic art, Scandinavian art, Eskimo art. Thus, differing cultures, in different places, at historical periods which differ, may produce similar designs in art. It is something I feel is common to all, not specific to any one individual.

For the moment, I may describe myself as an "Outsider Artist". I seem to fit the profile. And I like that, for now.

I have to date never sold any of my artwork, although I have given work away, or donated work for autism-related purposes, and I have had a book published featuring many of my pictures. And I have exhibited artwork many times, in the UK, Europe and the USA. Also I have given away thousands of prints to people I write to, know, friends.

Van Gogh apparently never sold any pictures while he was alive. Yet many would consider him a success. In any event his pictures today sell for millions. Picasso sold many pictures while he was alive, and he is considered a success too by many. And his work sells for millions too.

Success is a funny old thing. It may be achieving what one sets out to, or it may simply be as others see one. I suppose it is what one deems important, either oneself, or others.

I am not sure if I am a success. Sometimes I am successful, sometimes not. I know art fulfils a purpose in my life, and that in itself is success, and I am happy for that.

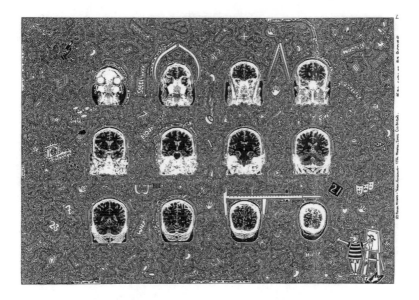

Peter lives in the UK and was diagnosed with Asperger syndrome just over ten years ago. His intricate and ornately patterned artwork is exhibited and published internationally. Even though Peter is computer illiterate, the comprehension and definition of his line drawings appear to have been produced by a computer. The beautiful, complex images serve as a rare window into the precision and creativity of an Asperger mind at work, or play, and which is which, when one could so easily be the other.

CHAPTER 16

AURAL SCULPTING – BEFORE AND AFTER

Colin Webber

My online user name in the various music, technology and Asperger forums I haunt is AuralSculpture. AuralSculpture as a person is not any different to me, just a convenient foil that allows me to be equal to every other forum member, be they amateur, student or, like me, an academic researching autistic traits and music. Aural sculpture is also a process – as a composer, I shape sound, moulding texture, carving line and form, using my ears to see the results. It is my very fortunate "special interest".

I have been a musician, composer and aural sculptor for most of my 42 years, but only for the last five or so have I been a conscious Aspie. For me there is a fairly clear distinction Before Diagnosis and After Diagnosis – my life "BD" and "AD". The diagnosis of residual Asperger syndrome started me on a path of study that has become my other (and frequently primary) "special interest". I have a long history of engaging in collaborative arts, usually cross-discipline or cross-culture, and had been studying this process in the few years BD.

By cross-discipline I mean working as a composer with related professionals, such as dancers and choreographers, theatre and film directors, actors and designers in multi-media collaborations, such as physical theatre and film. Each member of these teams has their own goals and specialisations, their own visions that combine to create the whole. As well as personality differences, sometimes generously proportioned egos and occasional clashes over practicalities, these members speak very different artistic languages, and have different modes of expression.

In my study BD I looked at the way communications flowed between myself and the other members of creative teams, and the musical responses I generated, comparing these against the reports and work of other practitioners. My investigation uncovered particular areas where anomalies were likely to arise, including group face-to-face creative meetings, a preference for written communications, "unique" musical responses to emotive content of a scene, procrastination against deadlines, satisfaction with the process rather than the result and a fascination with the directorial process with actors. I put these down to be areas of my personality and professional skill base that I could work on and improve.

Around the time this study concluded I was diagnosed with Asperger syndrome–residual. A child we knew had recently been diagnosed, and this started us thinking. It was pretty obvious really, once we knew what we were looking for, and certain aspects of life BD started to make more sense. And of course the research took a sideways step.

"What is the influence of these clear autistic traits on my music and creative work, in the past and in the present?" So this brief history brings me to the crux of this contribution. From a musical and personal point of view, does knowing make a difference?

The unequivocal response to that is "Yes", knowing makes a difference. Can I identify the influence that autistic tendencies have in my work and life? Absolutely. Sometimes. Maybe. Does the knowledge help make my life better? Well the jury's still out on that one too.

It is worth examining the idea of "residual" in relation to Asperger. The term is generally applied to adult Aspies and used to signify that the diagnostic criteria are met, but that the individual has developed sufficient coping mechanisms and work-arounds that the traits do not significantly impair normal functioning. The measures of significance and impairment are of course still open for professional debate, but what is clear is that autistic symptoms come in waves, and waves seem to come in tides, and tides also have their cyclical zenith. The height of these waves is certainly stress-related. It is also my observation that since diagnosis, and certainly while engaged in studying the subject, I appear to be somewhat *less* able to call on these coping mechanisms. I am certainly now able to recognise many of my "Aspie moments" for what they are, but unfortunately not yet while they are happening. Recognition after the event and anticipation of the next has become a constant source of anxiety, stress and depression, which then leads to deeper expression of traits.

It's a vicious cycle. There are many times that I wish for my previous life when I firmly believed that I was "right", "alright" and my course of action was the only one available. Those were days of certainty, days of blissful unawareness, but also days of dubious life decisions, lost and unformed friendships and deep and frightening chasms of the mind that would occasionally demand attention and all my will to ignore. Now there is no certainty. My constant companions are four questions: Am I perceiving this situation from a skewed, Aspie perspective? Am I allowing myself to be a victim of rigid thought? Did I get the social context or did I misunderstand? Which way am I going to screw up this time?

Since this contribution is meant to be about music, I guess that's enough background. There are lots of theories around the importance of music to the autistic mind. One has to do with logical and structural systems, another suggests a more direct connection to the brain's emotion centres. The relationship between music and maths is discussed at length; the regulatory influence of sonic rhythm on thought patterns and non-verbal language contexts are also the subject of study. My own observations are largely personal, but they fit quite nicely with some of these.

I call myself a composer or "aural sculptor" rather than "musician". I am uncomfortable in a performance environment – as the skills of my peers developed around me, it became too risky for me. I didn't want to practise enough to become a great performer – I preferred to compose.

In the mid-1980s I fell in love with the power of the recording studio and rode the wave of change that MIDI, synthesisers and computers brought about. Music technology gives the practitioner the ability to chase perfection in a more logical, cognitive way, to analyse each performance and tweak it "just so". It suits the control freak in me and gives me the opportunity to drill down into the minute details of a sonic world that I can lose myself in.

I love the detail! Sounds have their own worlds inside them, they grow, evolve, live, die over time, playing in the domains of frequency and timbre and space. I love to take the short sounds and make them long; the soft sounds and make them loud. I pile detail into my compositions, and then often have to take it out again to make them more palatable to others. Much of my music has a polyrhythmic freneticism that echoes the inside of my head. I am comfortable in the moment, but I struggle with longer form. The big picture requires a conscious left-brain planning session. Call it "weak central coherence", or more likely "enhanced local perception", if you like, but it works for me.

I have a tendency to labour the point sometimes. Sound familiar? I explore and push a single idea until it finds some kind of conclusion. This can work for me too. For example, I recently scored a short film about a young girl's first communion. It was set in the mid-sixties and there was some "source music" – music from the period playing on radios, etc. already in place. The film needed something to tie the scenes together and indicate the emotional journey of the character. At one point the priest is seen to wipe the communion vessel with a cloth, and this gave me the idea to use the sound of glassware for the score. I made many recordings of crystal glasses – rubbed, struck, swirled with water, and these became the source sounds for the music, beautiful tinkling bells, weird harmonic scrapings, and the church organ itself.

I mention here the concept of an emotional journey through the music. Emotional expression is not something that Aspies and autistics are generally known for, and the concept of an Aspie's empathic reading of a character might raise some eyebrows. But there's the thing – I find it much easier to understand a dramatic portrayal of an event, be it film or theatre, than a real one. It makes sense, dramatic portrayals are just that – portrayals. They are carefully designed events with many superimposed layers of clues. There is a constructed script that is quite different to "normal" conversation, even in so-called "naturalistic" work, a control of intent, a stripped-down focus of non-verbal activity. In the case of film, events unseen are shown, camera angles change, and point of view focuses on reactions. Even in a documentary, the "story" is told in a very defined way. As a composer, I also get to have discussion with directors and actors. I can have the emotional intent defined for me in words and test my own metaphoric meanings with them. I can discuss music they like, listen to their own musical tastes and ideas. Then I can surprise them. It is common for me to come back to a director with a musical response that is very unlike what they expected. For example:

Me – "Here you go, listen to this. This is 'fear'."

Director – "No, this is 'anger'."

Me – "Well, it frightens me!"

Director – "It has strength, power, it is the feared, not the fear itself."

Me – "Oh. OK, I'll have another go at it."

Director – "No, no, I love it! It will make the audience feel fear and empathise with the character."

Me – "If you say so!"

And so it goes, there is something to be said for an unusual response to emotional stimuli after all. I'm not attached to the piece – if the director wants to use it in a different way that is up to them. For me the process is more satisfying than the result.

The subject of working with directors brings me to another aspect of interest – collaboration. I have long been aware that the studio environment where I make much of my music with others is a place of great creative comfort for me. This is the place I am most trusting and open to other people's ideas. As a fairly rigid thinker, I generally have to force myself to deviate from intellectual paths and my "little rituals". However, once I hit the studio, whether the music is my own or I am producing someone else's work, I find myself very willing to be led on new ideas, sounds, creative paths by the other musicians. In fact I expect it. I don't want a session player to roll up and play the part as I wrote it – I'm looking for the players who will make the part their own, add their nuance, deviate from the path, play something else. I think there are two possible explanations for this. One has to do with the process mentioned above. The studio is a musical environment where talking about the music is encouraged. We play, we analyse, we discuss, we evaluate, we compare, and we play again. There is a strong cognitive engagement with what many consider a largely intuitive process so we can *think about how we feel* or, at least, I can. That separation of emotion and intellectual process comes in useful here. In the studio I get very involved. I sing along with the guitar solo, I leap around, I get excited. It's a very interactive and open environment and I feel like I'm a part of it – I feel. Even though others are mostly doing the playing, I feel like it's happening together. Which brings me to some more interesting research I stumbled across recently. When people make music together, particularly when they sing together, a brain chemical called oxytocin is released. Oxytocin is an interesting chemical known as the "trust drug" and more widely known to be released at key times such as childbirth, breastfeeding and orgasm – times when trust is built between the participants. It has been shown that giving oxytocin to autistics can increase social cognition, improve performance on empathy tests and reduce repetitive behaviours. It seems possible that something like this might be happening in the studio.

Researching something that in no small way defines the way you are is clearly a double-edged sword, inducing a paranoiac preoccupation with every thought, yet occasionally providing insight into past or present that would be impossible without subjecting oneself to "the literature". The biggest issue I find myself facing right now is figuring out how much of every waking (and dreaming) thought is actually relevant on a day-to-day basis. On balance, I'm glad I sought the help that culminated in a diagnosis. I'm glad I launched headlong into research, despite it being at times the opposite of therapeutic. Now if only we could persuade the rest of the world, the so-called neurotypical majority, to engage in some self-understanding, we just might get somewhere!

Dr Colin Webber is a composer, music producer and educator based in Brisbane, Australia. He has a lengthy list of credits in composition for theatre and dance, and has contributed music to a variety of TV and film productions. Since diagnosis a few years ago, he has been researching the ways in which his Asperger syndrome affects his composition work and especially his collaborative work with film and theatre makers. In his teaching of music technology, composition and audio production he frequently observes heightened autistic traits among his students and hopes to make some contribution to the community through understanding his own processes. He has recently acquired his doctorate; his research explored the impact of autistic traits on his own musical practice.

http://colinwebber.com

PART 5

SPECIAL INTERESTS

These three contributors talk about how their special interests led them to become specialists in their hobby fields.

With the gifts of specific focus, persistence and the love of detailed involvement, persons with ASD can be "specialists" and experts in whatever area is of their interest. They then crave the structured environment, the rules and predictability that go with the topic.

I don't know about you but I would rather discuss the ins and outs of someone's hobby at a party than their occupation – I may learn something new, and if I am listening to a person with ASD speaking about their hobby, I would *definitely* learn something new, unique and different about that topic.

You may call it obsessiveness, I call it brilliance!

- *Leith McMurray* discusses her musicality, and how it was introduced to her at a very young age and how her instruments and voice provided her with an anchor to get her through the years. She now realises it is due to her gift of Asperger syndrome that this has been such a positive path in her life.

- *Mark Boerebach* records the life events surrounding his intriguing gift of 80s music recollection and how the two go hand in hand. Read his contribution for a sentimental music trip back in time.

- *Will Hadcroft* describes in detail what it's like to use his fixations of sci-fi television to escape reality, and also how he personalised the shows to help him cope in the real world.

CHAPTER 17

MUSICALITY

Leith McMurray

I never knew my maternal grandfather and know very little about him as my granny booted him out not long after my mother was born. What I do know about him is he apparently had a fine singing voice, being an Irishman, but unfortunately was also fond of the drink. Mum was the third of three girls: Veronica (Vera), Aroha Treasure (*aroha* is the Maori word for "love") – known as Treasure – and Raemond.

Years later, a friend of the family came across my grandfather in some little country town in a remote area of the East Cape

(North Island, New Zealand) and was given a tidy sum "for the girls". This money had been won by gambling on the horses.

Granny spent the money on cultural education. The eldest daughter, Vera, had singing training. Treasure, the middle one, went to art classes but failed to develop any taste, and Rae, my mother, had dancing classes, which in retrospect seemed a bit odd, considering that she was by then losing her hearing (but she did very well). However, Vera developed a golden voice and was much in demand locally for radio broadcasts. She never grew very much due to a congenital hip problem, which also left her with a pronounced limp, but of course this didn't matter as no one could see her "on the radio" anyhow.

I give this side of my heritage the credit for my musicality, which was developed by my mother having had a taste of culture and found that it answered some yearning within her. My father, on the other hand, rigorously suppressed his musical leanings as he felt it would soak away too much of his meagre salary if he allowed himself to really enjoy music – buying records and so on (no concerts to go to in country towns in New Zealand in those days).

My father was a teacher and often said he could not bear being in the staff-room at morning teatime because of the buzz of voices. On the other hand, he was reasonably gregarious and busy in the community. My mother's deafness apparently caused her to be more introverted and socially awkward. Later, surgery restored her hearing to intolerable levels for her, and hyperacusis sensitivity then became a huge issue for her and me. It is only in retrospect that I wonder if it was the fact that the deafness was a convenient peg to hang everything else on, having no knowledge about Asperger syndrome in those days, that deafness became the accepted causal factor in her behaviour. At this point I must say that I am not sure from whom I inherited my Asperger syndrome. It may even have been from both parents!

When I was aged seven, my mother saved up and bought for me a brand-new piano and an excellent teacher was engaged. I stayed with Cecilia Worth for some years. She had been a violinist and once showed me her tiny violin, which she used as a child. I also had ballet lessons for a while, but the instructor kept changing the steps, or so I thought, leading to an unpleasant altercation, and that was the end of dancing! (This was Aspie insistence on being "right" in the face of the teacher's inability to understand why I couldn't understand her instructions – I was asked to leave, aged 8 years.)

I enjoyed singing at primary school, which was conducted over radio broadcasts to the schools. School music teachers at the primary stage were unheard of.

My mother took me to various musical/dancing shows in our main city, Hamilton, from time to time, which in retrospect was fairly unusual, given that we lived in a mining town (Huntly).

When I went to secondary school in a new town (Te Awamutu), there was a music teacher for me, Mrs Martin-Smith. In addition, there was a music teacher at the school, a very talented and deeply frustrated man called "Pooh-Bah" as a result of his having produced *The Mikado*. There was a school choir and yearly Gilbert and Sullivan operettas. I was up for everything and this was virtually the only area I could shine in. My musical education gave me an immediate advantage. Academically, I was a year younger than my classmates and tended to struggle (this was because I had been promoted on my reading abilities at the previous school, despite not having a good grasp of maths).

As I progressed through secondary school, I began entering in piano competitions during the school holidays. Here I really shone as a very able sight-reader, being able quickly to scan a previously unknown piece of music and to play it competently a minute or so later. I won quite a lot of prizes for that, even beating the hotshots from the big smoke on several occasions! At school, I spent my last year as School Pianist as all my "rivals" (favourites of Pooh-Bah) had left. This saw me playing as half of a two-piano orchestra for the school opera that year (*HMS Pinafore*).

In my hometown, when not at the piano competitions, I would volunteer to help at the singing competitions and was privileged to witness Malvina Major and Kiri Te Kanawa[1] in their student days and watch them improve to the point where their careers began to take shape. Of course, I heard much of the solo singers' repertoire and no doubt absorbed some technical skills as well. On one occasion, the accompanist for a "test piece" was late arriving, and I was drafted in to sight-read the accompaniment and then to play for all the children in this event. This allowed the programme to proceed as planned even though it was a very unusual solution!

I moved to Christchurch in my third year at university and my music took a back seat for some time. I had my piano in the house but didn't play it much. When my six-year-old announced that it was time she "learned about God", we trundled down to the local Church of England and very quickly I was playing the piano for the Sunday School and then also the organ for the church services. As well, several of the parents, including me, put together a small group using a small electronic keyboard, a guitar, various percussion instruments and singers, to play modern "choruses" before church services began. I think they were quite popular – we certainly enjoyed them!

I was lent an autoharp for a while and used that to accompany myself in singing and also to play for a children's singing programme at the local library one school holiday.

In 1986 I joined the Harmonic Society Chorale, a small chamber choir, for a year. When this folded I joined the parent Harmonic Society Choir and fulfilled a teenage ambition to sing the "Polovtsian Dances" from *Prince Igor* by Borodin, in the Christchurch Town Hall. I had heard the choir sing this on my little bedside radio years before and was enraptured. Singing with the big choir led to many appearances in the Town Hall, a most impressive modern performance space designed and built in 1972 with what was then the most modern acoustic design in the world.

---

1   Malvina Major and Kiri Te Kanawa both had stellar careers in international opera houses and both received the equivalent of a Knighthood from the Queen. They are now Dames!

Some of us travelled to Canberra, Australia, to celebrate the Bicentennial in a performance of Mahler's Eighth Symphony. The choir was so huge (about 800 people from all over Australia) we could have done with binoculars to see our conductor! We used the largest indoor space in Canberra at the time, the Bruce Stadium (an indoor basketball stadium). In the quiet intervals, we could hear the gents' WCs flushing automatically!

The Harmonic Society merged with the Royal Christchurch Musical Society, another "big" choir in 1990, because of falling audience numbers, making it difficult for both choirs to exist separately. Before the official merger, we travelled to Wellington, our capital city, to perform at the biennial Arts Festival in Verdi's *Requiem.* What a wonderful experience. The soloists were terrific and both our performances were sold out. Some years later we took part in another performance of Mahler's Eighth Symphony, with a dynamic young German conductor. Again, this was one of those indelible memories.

Thanks to my membership in the Harmonic Choir and the Christchurch City Choir, I have had 21 years of wonderful music and happy memories. This was not without a lot of struggle, however. The upside was continuing intellectual stimulation, both from the music and the learning challenges, and the friends I made over the years. The downside was the continued commitment to weekly practices over most of the year, more near the time of the concert, much frustration when things were not going well, and exhaustion after a particularly gruelling lead-up and performance. For the sesquicentennial of Christchurch we presented two "oratorios" in one night and practised (in addition to our months of preparation) every night for the preceding week. As I got older, this kind of commitment became harder to maintain. When I was feeling a bit depressed, which was often in those days, I found it really hard to get through a practice without crying. I'm not sure whether music unlocks feelings or whether it was just stressful. However, the choir also provided a predictable "anchor" in my life when other things were not.

The beginning of each year, after a six-week break, was often the most difficult for me and I would wonder why I was still participating in this masochistic exercise. Eventually, some spinal surgery led to my taking a complete break for some time, and I felt out of step when I returned. The music the choir was doing had fallen into a bit of a rut, and I was tired of hearing people being shouted at by the conductor. I felt stressed and anxious and no longer enjoyed it. I resigned, but go to most of the concerts, which I think I enjoy more than I did when singing in them!

I have tried a couple of smaller choirs, but one did not suit me and the other one took exception to an Aspie social solecism I committed and refused to have me back. One is much more under the spotlight in a small choir! However, I am a useful member of my church choir and also now play the organ on a rotational basis for services. This arrangement is increasing as I am seen as very capable of producing the desired musical support for services.

I love singing, both listening to it and singing myself. To me, it is the most direct expression of a person's innermost soul. Instrumental music is next best – soloists or small numbers, followed by orchestral music. The piano and the cello are my favourite instruments, but singing can be done without any accompaniment, anywhere, any time, and so is always available to us. Having said that, some of the world's greatest music is that written to accompany opera singers, and being enthralled by singing has led me to know a great deal of this music. I had a little bedside radio in my teenage years and listened to it frequently, beginning to know some of the great singers and music.

As an Aspie, I lack the ability to screen out unwanted sounds from my environment and I also suffer from volume issues (hyperacusis). Odd, in a way, that I would then enjoy large choir and orchestra combinations? Maybe Oliver Sacks could explain this better, but I will try. The music I enjoy is an organised and melodious combination of sounds. I have little time for "modern", atonal and apparently random clashing discords. There is, of course, beautiful modern music, which I do enjoy, where unusual chords and effects do produce a genuinely moving composition. Another important factor is that the kind of music I love is not artificially amplified. Music is something I know I am pretty good at, and over the years it has provided me with some much-needed positive feedback.

I felt my explanation of music was somewhat lacking, so asked a scientific friend, Brian Pryor, to provide some more information:

Scientists once thought the brain had two distinct processes: The logical, decision-making brain and the emotional brain. It now appears they believe we have an emotional brain which makes logic and rational decisions. So the processes are not separate. They coexist together. This is clearly illustrated with depression. Depression is a chemical imbalance. The neurotransmitter chemistry fails between nerve cells making simple everyday decisions difficult. Here the emotional brain has taken over the logical brain. [Interestingly, when I am depressed, the effort to sing is unbearable – I melt down completely.] Similarly, strokes and dementia are caused by the loss of dopamine, which affects movement, cognition and memory. Then, to make matters worse, we have two hemispheres. Not only do we have wiring problems; each hemisphere is meant to take on different tasks.

However, music can profoundly influence the brain. Normally we talk of left- and right-handed brain activity. Music is special. The eyes read the music score transferring it to both hemispheres simultaneously for processing into harmonies and rhythm from the memory. The information is then transferred as learned patterns to the fingers to play the notes. The ears receive the sound and it registers as similar to or the same as processed score and hopefully bathes the brain in a rewarding chemistry of success; all in all a wonderful cycle. Not only is it using all of the brain, it uses both hemispheres, and is monitored and adjusted to achieve the interpretation the player chooses and wishes to convey to the listener. It also has the effect of lowering the stress hormone serotonin, which relaxes the body to make more cortisone, which in turn repairs any damage. Music makes the brain happy. Music makes memories and sets up the neural pathways (the wiring) necessary to work well.

(NB: Playing an instrument such as a stringed or woodwind instrument involves reading only one line of music; however, if you are being accompanied, you will have either a keyboard rendition of the accompaniment to keep an eye on, or the lines of the other players, as not everyone will be playing simultaneously. If you are in an orchestra, you have to pay attention to the conductor, play your notes and count bars to make sure you come in at the correct place. An organist is effectively reading three lines of music as the feet are also involved! To do all this while keeping time, manipulating the stops to achieve different effects and also produce a musical performance is quite tricky!)

People often wonder if a conductor is really necessary; and certainly, some highly experienced small groups can play without a conductor. However, they will have a leader who gives the signal to start and finish, and in between will indicate very subtly other directions to the players. With an orchestra and a choir, a conductor is the glue that holds the ensemble together. A conductor indicates tempo (what speed), and changes in that; conveys the composer's expressive intentions; cues and "brings in" soloists; and is simultaneously reading from a huge musical score which contains all the instrumentation, a page at a time. Conductors will have annotated this score over many sessions of listening and practising, to remind themselves of particular emphases they want to make. This is an enormous intellectual challenge and may be a reason why conductors seem to live to a great age and still be able to carry out their musical tasks!

I guess it indicates that an Aspie ability to concentrate and pay attention to detail is almost a necessity when learning/playing music. Perfecting your performance (and enjoying it) is self-rewarding, as well as being a great way to experience success and praise, and be valued in a group! From my observations of other classical musicians, I would guess that a reasonably high proportion of them would be Aspie, and certainly some composers are thought to be or to have been so. Of course, if you are a musician in the first place, people "allow" you to be a bit different and eccentric.

There is a recent trend for younger people who become well known in New Zealand to refer quite naturally to their having Asperger syndrome, and in time I think this will be very helpful to all of us. As I look back on my life and see how AS has shaped it I am so grateful that I was given understanding before I am too old!

When Leith was a school child, music via the school broadcast lessons and hymns at church and Sunday school was almost the only music she would have heard apart from the home radio and piano lessons. At secondary school this broadened out both at school and from more access to concerts in Hamilton, her local "big city".

Leith was a "late bloomer", graduating with a Bachelor of Arts and Post-Graduate Diploma in Social Work at Canterbury University (New Zealand) in her thirties as a "mature student". However, chronic depression and anxiety have contributed to her difficulty in obtaining, and staying in, appropriate employment.

Leith was diagnosed with "Residual" Asperger syndrome five years ago, and is now in her early sixties.

Since her diagnosis and acquisition of knowledge and understanding of AS, Leith has set up a "peer-driven" social work, mentoring and counselling service for adult Aspies, in partnership with her equally musical Aspie friend, Jan Brooking. They have developed their own "Aspie-style" team-counselling approach, and find that it works well for their clients.

www.aspiehelp.com

CHAPTER 18

THE RECORDINGS OF A ROCK WIZ

Mark Boerebach

Of recent times I completed a music industry course, whereby my fellow students and teachers were intrigued about the way I could recall top of the chart songs so accurately. They were interested to know how I knew so much about eighties music, and why; as I simply told everyone – it was just the events of my life that made this possible.

Without trying to explain the formula of how I do this exactly, and bore everyone with a book of numbers and facts, about the size of Mt Kosciusko, I thought I would do a quick chronicle of the events that shaped my life, related to the songs that were popular for each time period, and how it also relates to my Asperger's, and various sensory experiences.

December 1979 saw The Buggles' "Video Killed the Radio Star" and ABBA's "Gimme! Gimme! Gimme! (A Man after Midnight)" reach the top of my charts. This was the time when we had our first swimming pool completed, just in time for Christmas.

For many years, I had a small red transistor radio, which by the end of July 1980 was on its last legs. My father travelled overseas and brought back a brand new mono radio-cassette recorder with some Maxell UL 90 cassettes. This was another impacting time in top 40 chart music, with "Can't Help Myself" by The Flowers (later called Icehouse), perhaps one of the best driving songs of all time.

On Saturday 11th April, I finally moved into my own room, and at this time I started my own fictitious radio station called 2VVX, which stood for Variety Variation eXtra. Though I got much joy out of it, my brother thought I was an idiot for talking into a radio-cassette recorder. At this time, I was listening to Air Supply's "Every Woman in the World".

The second week of the holidays saw my family, several friends and I go off to a huge waterpark. It seemed to be a day of much anticipation and excitement, until I hopped into one of the slides. For some reason, the stories I heard of people sticking razors into the tubes had freaked me out. Was this an Asperger's meltdown? I can remember being trapped halfway through the long pipe and balling my eyes out, I had never felt so scared in my entire life.

It's now October 1981, a period when I discovered I was dreaming of another planet. As you could say, I was living two lives, the one I lived during my waking hours, and a strange but interesting one while asleep; a place called Earth 2. The dream would generally consist of my progression through life, toward being an astronaut, running a space agency, establishing a media network, owning a soft-drink company, running record companies, and owning a media empire. At this particular time, I dreamt of being a DJ on a music station called "Super Rocket Music". During this month, I would be listening to Olivia Newton-John's "Physical" and Cliff Richard's "Wired for Sound".

By late March 1982, my Asperger syndrome and several small things were about to come together. The lava was flowing, and it would only take something small to happen to pop the volcano. Not in an angry outburst, but more into a major emotional breakdown, and a severe loss of confidence. My teachers were already getting concerned about the fact that my comprehension projects were repeated failures. My parents were also getting very concerned at the amount of time I would spend taping songs off the radio, and the number of blank tapes I would go through. The reality that I couldn't do simple things like tie shoelaces, cross the road, go to the local grocer to get bread or milk, or even cut a slice of bread from a loaf that father would bring home from his work was becoming very worrying, as if my development suddenly went back four years.

Having Asperger's meant that my perception of certain things was way out of proportion, meaning that I thought that the Panasonic cassette recorder I had was worth thousands of dollars. By April 1982, the unit had had several months of extremely heavy use. In the early hours of Thursday 1st April, it finally chewed its first cassette, which triggered the thought that I had ruined an expensive piece of equipment. This would be the final blow. The reaction wasn't instant as I got through that day of school without any problem; the following evening I cried for hours in the darkness of my room, without telling anyone how I felt.

My failures with the comprehensions at school were due to the rules where the papers could only be read once. The Asperger's would make the gathering of details difficult when reading something the first time. Because there was more emphasis on my vision, the failures were put down to me being stubborn and not wearing my glasses. My inability to tie shoelaces was because the Asperger's mind has difficulties in taking in certain instructions of dexterity. When it came to crossing roads, judging the distance of cars would be difficult, which meant I would actually wait until there weren't any cars. I would often stand on the footpath for ages, as those moments wouldn't happen often. The simple task of buying a bottle of milk would be like trying to find a bottle amongst a circus of colours, as all the various milks had different packaging.

Though none of the issues were addressed, there was a marked improvement with my schoolwork during July 1982. Some of my favourite television shows at the time were the first season of *Fame*, *Countdown* and a revived version of *Pick a Box*. I was still filling up the blank tapes with the hits like Bucks Fizz's "My Camera Never Lies".

It's now November 1982, a point where I had received mobility training from an itinerant teacher, Janet. She would teach me how to cross roads, catch buses and trains, buy groceries, etc. Thursday 11th was the day when she tested my skills – unaware of my Asperger's, she would follow me from about 100 metres behind, supervise me crossing roads, approaching the train station, checking my train pass and the indicator boards, then watch me catch the train. Some streets were no problem to cross as they were quiet streets; however, others would be full of cars. The prospect of negotiating traffic and judging distances of moving cars would already be a challenge enough for a vision-impaired person. The reality of judging when to cross initiated a severe meltdown, causing me to cry for several minutes. Again, it was assumed I couldn't see the traffic, because I wasn't wearing my glasses. Both my itinerant teacher and class teachers were very upset and annoyed. After this, it was assumed that I didn't want to be a mobile person, and my training was dropped. At no point was there any consideration that the Asperger's mind was dealing with information overload, and even worse there could have been a fatality. It seemed that Janet was unable to adapt to the different needs of the various special needs students.

It's now Friday 24th December 1982, when my parents put on a large Christmas party for all our relatives, and their employees. Cartridges from the Intellivision were on Santa's list that year, as I got "Lock 'n' chase" and "Mission X". My cousins and I were playing those games for hours, when I had then become somewhat thirsty. Going to the fridge, I pulled out a bottle of lemonade. In those days, soft-drink bottle designs were different. The transparent plastic was much softer and thinner, and glued to the bottom was a black plastic dish, which was also made of a very thin soft plastic called polypropylene. As I was about to pour the lemonade, I noticed an intense reaction inside my body. I suddenly went into a deep sense of euphoria, which gave me the urge not to squeeze the bottle, but to place my hand over the black dish on the bottom, and gently squeeze my fingers into it. This would cause both the transparent and black plastic to bubble in and out. This gave a certain soft bubbly texture, which for some unknown reason had initiated an emotion that would generally head off into the direction of total euphoria.

It's now Thursday 3rd February 1983, my first day at high school, a time when The Little River Band was charting with "The Other Guy". The first two minutes of high school was going into a staff-room to collect a timetable, in which at that same moment my bag with all my new books, pencils and lunch was stolen. It would be found a few days later, covered in urine and dirt. With already being bashed against the wall on the first day, it wasn't a good start to high school, but it was unfortunately the sign of things to come.

On a cool rainy Sunday March afternoon, all my relatives and cousins came to celebrate my brother's 21st birthday. It was more cushion fights in my bedroom, as the tunes played on the radio. Joe Cocker and Jennifer Warnes' "Up Where We Belong" title had some kind of special meaning, as the teasing at school continued, and at night I would go "up where we belong" to Earth 2. The escapism to this place helped me deal with the roughness that was all around.

Through June the bullying continued hard and rough at my high school, with the teachers not caring less. During 1983, we did various craft subjects, then at the beginning of term two, sewing with a class of 20 boys and 10 girls. Obviously the boys mucked up, and the few interested girls brought some old clothes to practise on, but it seemed that the teacher was actually not just concerned for my emotional welfare, but also cared about my safety. She would often let the pupils do their work, while I was able to tell her about the problems I had in the playground. Though she cared, the corrupt nature of the high school meant that her compassion had no impact on any of the other staff.

Wednesday 17th August 1983 was a cool, very wet, and dark day at school, as the cloud cover was extraordinarily heavy. Ironically it was perhaps one of the best days I remember. One of the bullies from the special unit was sitting near me during my art class. As it was my last day, before going on holidays for over a month, it was the perfect opportunity to "return the medicine". I had politely asked the teacher if I could leave early. Upon letting me go, I punched the kid very hard in the head. He became angry at an urge to retaliate as quick as he could, but with him being held back by the teacher, I left in a hurry, and ran up the stairs that would take me to the top floors of the school, where there'd be less congestion. I sped through one of the hallways, and then fired myself through another that was well over a hundred metres long. Jumping down the stairs, I saw him in the far distance of the hallway, but knew if I kept it up that I would get away. Around the home economics rooms I darted, and through the alcove, past the special unit, down the eastern quad, and finally, the car park, where my taxi was waiting. Already in there were my other two friends from the special unit. Upon closing the door, the windows were covered in raindrops, and that kid jumping on top, trying to open the door, only for the rain to make him slip off. The taxi driver pulled out onto the road with me feeling somewhat nervous. With much relief the bullying kid slid away, and would have much to contemplate over the coming month. As he lived on the other side of Sydney, I had nothing to fear.

Upon getting home, I had a shower, and started preparing my bags for our trip to Holland the next day. It was now the big occasion, going overseas for the first time. I watched *Towards 2000* that night, then taped more tracks off the radio.

I was excited about having a window seat, as being up in the clouds would give me a closer sense of being on Earth 2. I thought being on a flight for over 24 hours would give me much spiritual connectivity with my Earth 2 dream. An argument between my brother and mother brought a quick end to that one. For some reason, the 12-inch version of INXS's "Black and White" was stuck in my head for the entire trip, including the ten-hour delay at Bangkok.

On arriving back home a month later, my brother and I hooked up my new Philips to my radio corner, as I started recording the first few songs onto a TDK SA 90 cassette. I remember taping Mike Oldfield's "Moonlight Shadow" again, and the shear beauty of hearing such a nice piece of music in stereo. The haunting sounds of Maggie Reilly's voice had transitioned me for moments into my Earth 2 trip, moments that I found rather haunting, but beautifully relieving from the problems I would soon face again, when going back to school.

My confidence for crossing roads during June 1984 was still at a low point. However, it seemed having the right kind of instructor would pave the way for change. From June onwards, my road-coach, Julie, took me to the local intersection down from the high school, where I practised using the pedestrian crossing. She watched as I walked around five times, without being rushed or pushed. She had then asked how I felt about it, and said that I could practise in my own time, then to let her know when I was ready for the next lesson. Though at first I took the lazy way out and didn't practise, her lack of aggression and pushiness was enough to boost my confidence. Though I had left the exercise for weeks, in late September I went to the local news agency to get the paper for my parents, something I'd never done before. With no fear, I was now able to cross the roads near our place. I guess looking back at this scenario: the patience of Julie had brought results, as the pushiness of Janet was a recipe for immediate failure and a possible fatality.

The bullying at high school continued in 1985, but it was a time when I would discover that the technique with the plastic soft-drink bottles I mentioned earlier would come in handy to assist in managing the emotional trauma I suffered. Though the activity had a strange nature about it, going through the motions of such an activity would relax my hands, then my body, and ultimately place me into a deep sense of euphoria. It was a thought process that had already sparked during Christmas 1982, but at the time it was something I never took seriously. It was Tuesday 9th April 1985, when some of my relatives came over to celebrate Easter. Upon pouring a drink for my cousin, I was about to dispose of the large plastic soft-drink bottle. I wrapped my hand around the large black plastic dish on the bottom and felt an immediate sense of relief, alleviation and pleasure.

I got into the habit of cleaning the plastic bottles when they were empty. Rather than just crushing them, I would grab the bottom section by placing my hand over the black dish portion. Upon squeezing, the thin plastics would have a bubbling reaction, which had then placed me into a deep sense of pleasure and ease.

During May through to September, the bullying activity had increased to such a high level that I could have become suicidal if I had not had any coping mechanism. At this time, my family consumed much soft drink, which meant there was always an empty bottle around. When I was being bashed during lunch or during a period, I would concentrate on the fact that I would focus that anger upon getting home when I was able to squeeze another bottle, which was a great way of relieving that anger inside.

Though the strategy was a 100 per cent success, it was something that I would tell no one, because the concept of such an activity was strange and unusual. I just thought that if it worked, then why question it? Though things were rough during this period, I remember feeling good and mostly on top of it.

It is now September 1985, the point at which I turn 16. Not only would I be another year older, it was the age in which I would start receiving a pension for being visually impaired. I came home on Thursday 24th October 1985, with my parents showing me a cheque that had arrived in the mail from social security. As this was the time when my interest in music further increased, it was a time when I would buy more records and CDs. This would end up to be a potent cocktail that would eventually place my parents and me at virtual war. With my parents wanting me to save money, I would often go behind their back to the local shopping centre and buy CDs. It would get to such a level by 1987 that, a few times, my parents would make me take the discs back.

My dreams of Earth 2 started becoming much more regular again during October 1985. At this time, I would dream of being Earth 2's first man to go to Mars. At night after dinner, I would often sit in my bedroom corner unit, with the lights off, moving my body to the shaking motions of a launching rocket, as the communications went to the control centre, something like NASA's Houston complex. It was kind of taking my imagination away from the problems that I was so entrenched in at school.

1986 would start off to be a great year, as I would score great passes in English. It seemed after so many years at high school I would find a teacher that genuinely had my well-being at heart. She was very concerned about the amount of bullying I received, and would allow me to sit completely separate from the troublemakers. She was also liberal with marking, and would often give good feedback to my parents. Aside from my English, my marks for Art would also skyrocket, as by year's end I became the top student in that class.

It was also at the end of this year that I performed my first work experience at Australia Post. 1987 and 1988 were years that became very difficult, as there would be much studying with the coming of the end of year certificate. It would always be a struggle between listening to my records and cassettes, and my parents pulling me away to put more effort into studying. Though it was somewhat too late, I finally understood the importance of my HSC, and studied hard. The tension and the tests all came in October, and on Tuesday 8th November 1988 I sat my last exam.

Upon getting home that afternoon, I jumped into our swimming pool with all my clothes, and shouted "Hooray!" at the top of my voice, "No more home-work or studying!" After coming out, I celebrated the moment with playing Dragon's version of "Celebration", which originally was a hit for Kool and the Gang in 1981. With the exuberant moods aside, it was soon time for me to realise that I was on the threshold of the next stage of my life. The secure days of going to school were over, and now it was time to face the serious prospect of working in the open employment market.

Besides entering a new stage of life, I was also facing another unsettling reality. For several years I found squeezing the black dish portion of the larger plastic bottles to be a great relief. In August 1989, I started to discover that all the soft-drink companies were making changes. The soft bubbly "black dish" portion of the plastic bottles was replaced with new thickened rocket bottoms. Rather than feeling paper thin, these new rocket bottoms were as hard as thickened glass, and now were of no use to me. The new reality that there was now no rescuing relief from a tense situation was a major emotional worry. Consequently, because I was bullied and ridiculed during my first job as a trainee clerk, it finally led to me having a nervous breakdown during 1991–1992. Without those soft plastic bottles to emotionally stimulate me, one of my brothers saved me from a near possible suicide. This was when I was sitting on the edge of a lookout near our house in the Blue Mountains in August 1991.

The TAFE (Technical and Further Education) portion of the traineeship was a major success as I had graduated with passes for office admin. This was followed by my acceptance at a private college where I studied computer operations, resulting in a diploma pass in June 1991. With my efforts in finding paid work, I found short-term employment. This would be a data operating position and then a radio announcer job at 2BLU FM. With getting more experience, I then started doing more regular broadcasts for Sydney West Radio during the middle part of 1992. The station was an unlicensed aspirant at first, but gave me the chance to train up my radio station, and program production skills.

1993 was another busy year, as I recorded more radio programs. I started researching more of my music charts during this time, which led to me hosting a variety of programs on Sydney West Radio during June and September. I was responsible for getting the station sponsorships, and filling in air slots. During this time I completed a course at Blacktown TAFE on desktop publishing.

Though I kept as busy as possible, my Asperger's meant that finding paid work was still rather difficult. During this time, I would find much inspiration and motivation from my Earth 2 dream, as this was the source for much of my art. Though I would get myself involved with as much as possible, there was always a lack of something when not in regular work, a lack of being with other people, and the learning experiences that being with others would bring.

By September 1993, the community radio station had grown, with more airtime and a larger transmitter, which gave me the opportunity for more shows, and to play various music styles. By 1994, I aired a show every few weeks. My time was also devoted to completing another telemarketing course, as I thought the perfect job for me would be working in directory assistance.

Though the nature of the tasks was repetitive, it would have suited my Asperger's abilities in the aspect of it being a routine job.

1995 saw my involvement in Sydney West Radio grow as I commenced work on the station's newsletter. By the end of the year, my programming status was raised to a slot every Saturday. At this point the station's transmitter had the potential of covering 1.5 million people, and I was now enjoying my radio hobby very much. At this point I made some other friends, and found that the Saturday-down-to-the-radio-station routine was a nice break from the quietness of where we lived.

By the mid-1990s I had completed a six-month work experience at a neighbourhood centre. This was the time when my involvement at Sydney West Radio was at its peak, when I successfully closed a deal for getting the local printers to run the station's newsletter off. I was also compiling charts, records and CDs, producing sponsor announcements, organising the program schedules, negotiating programming slots, liaising between record companies, and organising voice talent for voice-overs and sponsor announcements. Unfortunately, the management of the radio station had no understanding of my Asperger syndrome, which led to my program being dropped, and ultimately me leaving the station. Though I left with a heap of good friends, the management seemed to have suffered from the tall poppy syndrome. As much as it was disappointing, my attitude was to just carry on, and find something new.

It was now 1998, the dawning of the internet era. I had amassed something in the vicinity of 1500 hand-written music charts, that all had to be converted into digital documents for easier retrieval. Over a period of nearly two years, I worked on my charting project. This involved the scanning, retyping, and archiving of every individual music chart.

I started researching the internet from about April 1999, and investigated the chances of starting an internet radio station. In 2000 the first album reviews were created, as I then tested out some preliminary websites. These were only free webhosting services, but it was good enough for me to learn and evaluate how the creation of websites worked. In late 2000, Planet Retro had opened, which listed reviews of my favourite albums. By early 2001 the first technical tests for uploading programs were carried out. During this period internet technology rapidly improved, and in June I finally got my own computer. This meant I was able to install my own sound production software, and by August create the first test radio program.

On Monday 26th November 2001, Planet Retro had transmitted its first radio program. It was a 30-minute mix of some eighties music, including Olivia Newton-John's "Xanadu" and some other retro hits. I had never felt so good as that night, with my own internet radio station making its first recorded test to the world. Unfortunately the website was on a free server, which meant there were several limitations.

In August 2002, I had finally moved out of home, and into my own place. Though it was scary at first, it was a strange feeling being able to spread my wings. I had never felt so free. The bittersweet reality was though that I was now responsible for all my own actions, such as the washing, cooking and anything else that came with living by oneself, including paying the rent and bills.

Thursday 31st October 2002 is perhaps a day I will remember for reaching another one of my personal goals. It was the re-launch of Planet Retro, but more importantly, the switch to a paid host, and the launch of 2PR FM internet radio. Now living in my own flat, and operating my own internet station, I felt like some kind of king. Though I completed the most important thing, moving to a paid host, which freed me from several broadcasting limitations, there were many more things to sort out, such as how my listeners were going to tune in, what media player I was going to use, how I was going to handle copyright, and other hosting issues. With all this bubbling away, I never gave up looking for paid work.

Though my radio station was a great help in keeping me occupied, the long period of unemployment still took a toll on my emotions. I realised that this would only mean that I would just sink down unless I addressed my attitude in life. From the reality of nearly having another nervous breakdown from the sheer struggle of living off unemployment benefits, I had found new hope in immersing myself into my Earth 2 dream. Though I had drawn several pictures, they would mean nothing, unless I started writing about them. From September 2003, I dropped everything, and for a few weeks started memorising everything that I could about Earth 2, and placing it down in point form. A week later, I would start writing it down in novel format, and within the space of a few weeks had already put down a few dozen pages.

With my radio station and novel in tow, I thought it would be an idea still to keep myself involved with some more courses. In 2005 I completed a 12-month course that resulted in learning about the Adobe Creative Suite package, and receiving a certificate II pass in pre-press graphic design.

Upon starting the various classes, I discovered that one of the teachers had a young son with Asperger's. With so many things in common, my teacher and I bonded, as he was very impressed with my recall of chart hits from the 1970s and 1980s. As I progressed through the lessons, he and my fellow students thought it would be a great idea for me to try out for one of Australia's popular quiz shows called *RocKwiz*. As my teacher also trained in film production, he filmed my journey from starting my course, the TAFE barbecue for raising the money, through to the plane trip to Melbourne, where the filming for *RocKwiz* took place.

Along the way, I was also tested by the declared rock-brain of the universe, Glenn A. Baker. He was so impressed with my music knowledge while visiting his place that he'd declared me the new pop-brain of the universe. I kind of laughed at it at first, as the reality was somewhat surreal, but in the end it was an experience and a half, and just a whole lot of fun. Upon looking around his place, I was totally mindblown by the amount of records and CDs that were strewn around, so many that I accidentally walked on and tripped over them when getting around his house. With my parents thinking that I was always obsessed with buying music, they should have seen this guy's place, I was no match for this music maniac of Australia.

It was now October 2008, and both my documentary and filming of *RocKwiz* were finished. The last week of October came, the week when both shows were due to go to air on SBS. My teacher and his wife, who was involved with a Sydney Asperger's support group, did much work behind the scenes. Within the one week I had two newspaper and four radio interviews, and an appearance on the national television news. For so many years being unrecognised, my moment in the bright glare of fame was now here. Even a day later, when attending my classes at TAFE, three people said that they'd seen the documentary on television.

It was now Saturday 25th October. Though I knew who won the show, as it had already been taped in July, the rest of Australia, and for that matter the rest of the world, was about to find out. It was a trip down the south coast, to spend the night with my family, and for that celebratory party. With my relatives and parents sitting around the lounge-room, the lights went down as Bryan and Julie introduced themselves on *RocKwiz*. The show gathered its momentum, and as my family gasped, there I was on television. Question upon question went past as I answered with much vigour. The minutes flew past, and before I knew it, my team and I were victorious, as my family cheered me on. The goalpost was reached, as my musical knowledge gave me the edge, and did it feel good to be the new rock-brain of *RocKwiz*.

Though it didn't get me paid work straight away, I felt my world open up, with many new friends, and as of September 2009 another one of my goals was reached. 2PR FM had conducted its first successful live broadcast test, a month-long broadcast with my home unit being the studio. A few friends contributed their programs, and the seed for 2PR FM being a full-time live broadcaster was planted.

Mark was diagnosed with autism at the age of three, and reassessed in 1976 with Asperger syndrome. Despite difficulties with social environments, he has achieved many of his goals, with only 20 per cent vision in one eye. Aside from having a flair for pastel arts, he has accomplished the successful completion of several courses, and the establishment of his own internet radio station – 2PR FM. This is where he's able to exploit his encyclopedic knowledge of the Australian top 40 charts.

CHAPTER 19

SCI-FI REALITY

Will Hadcroft

"Oh, that's not because you've got Asperger's," I'm told. "We all do it. The men have their football and the women have their soaps." But are these things really the same as what I do with my programmes? The men love football and think about it a lot, sure; the women follow their soaps and know all the storylines. The men meet up with one another and get the drinks in when there's a match on, while the women chat about the latest instalment over the phone.

But are they doing what I am doing? Do they record and keep every single match, every single episode, and watch them again and again? Do they recount details of events to themselves? Do they understand the processes behind the production of *Match of the Day*? Do they know who composed the theme music and designed the title sequence?

Most of the women I work with love *Coronation Street*. But how many of them know that it'll be a good episode if Daran Little has scripted it? How many of them even notice the names of the writers?

I am different, and it is because I have Asperger syndrome. My whole personal history is characterised by sounding and looking like everyone else and yet being slightly out of synch with the world at large. In the world, but not of it, as a wise man once said.

So, why do these people insist that it's nothing to do with Asperger's? I think it is down to one of two things. They are keen to reassure me that I'm like them, I'm "normal"; or they resent my assertion to being different, even subtly different (because possibly in their minds different may mean superior), and reject the claim.

It is assumed the geeks and nerds of society are, one and all, obsessed with computer programming and addicted to *Star Trek*. But this is a generalisation, and like all generalisations it is made by those who watch from a distance and do not really understand the drive behind such fixations. If it were as simple as "computers and *Star Trek*", psychologists would have had an easier time understanding and defining the Asperger condition long ago.

One of my dearest friends loves computers, so much so that he even thinks up new equations and programs when he's relaxing on the beach! He likes science fiction generally and is perhaps a little shy when meeting new people, but I wouldn't say he's on the autistic spectrum. Computers and science fiction by themselves do not equal Asperger syndrome.

For me, while I do like science fiction generally, there are only four television programmes that I fixate on, and in each case it is because I see elements of myself in them. Over the years

I have been able to use these programmes for solace, comfort, inspiration and (perhaps most importantly) escape.

DOCTOR WHO

At the time of writing, BBC Television's *Doctor Who* is enjoying popularity not witnessed since the height of Tom Baker's reign in the late 1970s. The nameless enigmatic Doctor tumbling through time and space in his TARDIS (Time And Relative Dimension In Space) is thrilling youngsters and their parents once again.

The programme was originally conceived in 1963 as a children's adventure serial for the winter months and centred around the character of the Doctor, who was manifest as a bad-tempered old man on the run from his own race. Veteran actor William Hartnell played the part until 1966 when he became too ill to continue, and the production team risked re-casting the part. Due to the flexible nature of the series, the metamorphosis of the Doctor could be explained within the narrative as "regeneration". Patrick Troughton agreed to become the Second Doctor on the understanding that he would completely reinterpret the role his own way. And so the crotchety old man became a scruffy eccentric boffin. Audiences embraced the transformation and the series' longevity was secured.

Today the series is as popular as ever, with the Doctor having reached his 11th incarnation.

Doctor Who refuses to die, and the reason for that, in part, is the obsessive mindset of its devotees. In 2003, *Doctor Who Magazine* ran a feature entitled "The Fan Gene". Its author, Gary Gillatt, had looked into the subject of autism and discovered its milder cousin Asperger syndrome. He examined the diagnostic criteria and was intrigued at how the stereotypical *Doctor Who* fan fits the description. Some fans were enraged. Personally the article surprised me, but in the end it set me on the road to finding answers to questions that had perplexed me for years.

You see I had always had this feeling that I was somehow a little different to my peers. I felt as though I was in a separate groove to everyone else, rowing my boat in the opposite direction, always on the outside looking in.

When I hit secondary school, I could not cope with the sudden change in speech and behaviour, and what I perceived as superficial attempts on the part of my peers to fit in and be accepted. It seemed to me that they would say and do anything to win the favour of their classmates. I had no such desire, and I could not understand what it was that drove them. I wanted to be liked, of course I did, I wanted to be popular – but not at such a high price. I wanted to be liked for being me. I had no interest in reinventing myself just to gel with the unwritten but mutually agreed rules of school life.

Paradoxically, I could see that I was liked by many of them, and I did have a best friend for most of the time I was there. Yet I still sensed that I was looking at the world through a sheet of glass. I could hear them and see them, and vice versa, but I wasn't with them at all. I suffered feelings of loneliness, and at times despair. *Doctor Who* was my escape route.

The character of the Doctor is motivated by an intense desire to right wrongs and protect the underdog. He fled his home world for reasons best known to him, and on the few times we've seen him in the company of his own people, he is barely able to hide his contempt and cannot wait to get away from them. Although he has a travelling companion, the Doctor is always self-contained, a closed book in some respects, and slightly melancholy. He can never settle.

All of this is potent stuff to the Aspie child, and it certainly was in my case. The Doctor kind of mirrored who I was, and on another level reflected the kind of person I wished I could be. Nothing ever seemed to faze him!

My obsession with the character peaked when Colin Baker debuted as the Sixth Doctor in 1984. I was 14 then, and while I had settled as best I could at school, I still felt at odds with the world, as though I had fallen to earth from somewhere else and was stuck here. The Sixth Doctor was the most alien of them all. He seemed to care little about how his observations and judgements would be received by others. He was impatient with his companion Peri and condescending to practically everybody. He didn't seem to be able to help himself, his tone of voice implying aloofness and pomposity, and his dress sense was appalling.

Actor Brian Blessed once noted that this Doctor never seemed truly happy, his smile not quite completing. At 14, I had spotted this too. The Doctor was on a plane singularly his own. Colin Baker himself said that he imagined the Doctor to be so removed from the everyday and so deeply affected by hundreds of years of time/space travel that he might stride over a pile of dead bodies and be unconcerned, and then weep at the death of a butterfly.

I left school in 1986 and was thrown into the working world with no real idea of what it was going to be like. The truth, namely that it was just an adult version of school, had a profound effect on me, and I recoiled even further into my *Doctor Who* cocoon.

The Doctor returned that autumn, and, as with the previous season, I recorded the whole lot on video, and watched it whenever I had the opportunity. If the family went out on a day trip, I would stay at home and watch my Time Lord hero, the only person I truly identified with – and he wasn't even real. My mother was at her wits' end when she heard me reciting whole scripts to myself, sitting on the edge of my bed or staring out of the kitchen window. I often felt on the verge of insanity.

It's funny, though, how things come full circle. In 2005 I published my autobiography *The Feeling's Unmutual* and tracked down Colin to see if he would endorse it. He had been one of the people angered by Gary Gillatt's article and its suggestion that some of the more eccentric fans might have Asperger syndrome. My story fascinated him, especially since what had so infuriated him had actually helped me gain relief. An explanation for my past: Asperger syndrome. Colin did indeed endorse my book and we have exchanged many an email since. He has told me things about his own school days and it appears we have some things in common as real people. And to think, he was my boyhood hero, my escape from this false world.

While I no longer need it in order to be happy, I confess I think about the original *Doctor Who* series every day.

THE INCREDIBLE HULK

I'm not talking about the comic book created by Stan Lee and Jack Kirby in 1962, nor am I referring to the big screen movies of this 21st century. To me, *The Incredible Hulk* is Bill Bixby as Dr David Banner with body builder and former Mr Universe Lou Ferrigno as his fury personified, in the Universal Television series created by Kenneth Johnson spanning 1977–82.

Initially, the appeal for me was the same as it was for every other child in Britain: I just wanted to see Banner get beaten up, transform into the Hulk, and throw the bad guys about. But as I got older and as I had more and more confrontations with the bullies, and certainly as I made the transition to secondary school, I began to identify closely with the human side of the character.

I didn't handle anger very well. I never swore at anyone, I very rarely got physical, and I certainly didn't get into fights or get into trouble. I didn't even make cruel remarks. But inside I was often enraged. Frequently the butt of jokes in the first couple of years of secondary school because of my shyness, I longed for an overdose of gamma radiation so I could vent my rage.

A visual aid from *The Incredible Hulk* helped here. It was from the main title sequence in which Banner is trying to undo a wheel nut on his car and change a flat tyre. The lug wrench slips and he smashes his hand on the road. An intense sound effect signals the onset of the metamorphosis. We go into his blood stream where his adrenalin rushes, and then into his DNA where one of the cells is glowing. David's eyes turn from brown to white, his clothes burst under the impact of his swelling muscles, and his face adopts an animalistic countenance. The Creature is the embodiment of Banner's rage.

The imagery of the white eyes and glowing DNA rooted themselves into my psyche, and at the moment my own anger peaked I would recall those scenes, sometimes mimicking vocally the high-pitched sound effect and dramatic music.

Tabloid reporter Jack McGee, a man obsessed with identifying and exposing his "John Doe", pursues Banner. One of the main factors in enabling audiences to suspend their disbelief was the pathos surrounding David Banner. Following each transformation and reversion, he is consumed with guilt and a genuine sorrow. Indeed, on occasion he actually breaks down in tears. Every episode concluded with Banner moving on, wandering down a wilderness road to Joseph Harnell's "Lonely Man" piano theme. Again, potent stuff for any depressed teenager.

I revisited *The Incredible Hulk* when it was repeated briefly in Britain circa 1988. By this time I was approaching my twenties and still struggling with social skills. Depression was a very present part of my life. When I watched an episode called "The Psychic", I was touched by the scene in which Banner contemplates suicide, convinced that the curse is no longer the Creature he turns into, but rather the man he has become. I watched the episode more times than is healthy for someone suffering from severe melancholia.

Today, the writings of Kenneth Johnson have inspired my own children's book series *Anne Droyd*.

THE TRIPODS

This is set one hundred or so years into the future but it looks like England at the dawn of the Industrial Revolution – that was my first impression. Villagers gather to celebrate Jack's big day. He has turned 16 and is about to cross the threshold into adult life. The crowd fall silent and look on in reverent awe as the giant alien Tripod stands in the village pond. The boy is plucked from the ground and placed inside its steel belly.

He is then returned a man. The villagers applaud as he removes his trilby, his shaved head now exhibiting the wire mesh of the Cap. Woven into his scalp, it will be part of him until the day he dies.

Amidst the crowd are two 15-year-old cousins. They go on the run and, with a French boy whom they nickname Beanpole, travel to the White Mountains (Swiss Alps) where a community of un-Capped free thinkers are plotting to destroy the controlling aliens.

Initially, the television series was a success and my schoolmates loved it. Then it dawned on them that, while it might be called *The Tripods*, there were not going to be that many Tripods actually in it, as Will, Henry and Beanpole were repeatedly captured and threatened with Capping. Audiences soon got their kicks from watching *The A-Team* on the opposing channel, but I stuck with *The Tripods* because I thought I could see parallels with the real world.

It seemed to me that a great many people at school, pupils and teachers, and a great many people in the wider world, were Capped. The education system claimed to foster individualism and creativity, but I believed that it was having the opposite effect, pushing young minds into pigeonholes, fashioning them to be what it believed they should be. Only a tiny handful of youths and teachers were genuinely unaffected, I decided, and naturally I was one of them.

As the story progresses, Will and his friends explore a decimated Paris before becoming guests at a lavish chateau. There Will falls in love with the enchanting Eloise and is even persuaded to marry her — until she wins a beauty contest and is taken, willingly, to serve the Tripods in their City of Gold. Even this struck a chord with me, since I had been hankering after a girlfriend that would see the world the way I saw it. There were none to be found. Girls were impressed with fashions and trends, clothes, make-up and boys who were cool. I believed these to be grossly superficial. I was desperate for female companionship, but not at that price.

When Series One climaxed, I immediately went out and bought the books on which the programme was based. I soon discovered to my delight that the trilogy was much faster-paced and was very easy to read. The back cover blurb declared, "John Christopher's almost unbearably exciting trilogy in one volume." I certainly could not argue with that.

Series Two was better paced, and the episodes set inside the City of Gold were gripping. But the programme was beaten in the ratings by shows on the opposing channel. Eager to save money, BBC1 Controllers Michael Grade and Jonathan Powell cancelled the third and final series. I was absolutely gutted by the news, and personalised the defeat. BBC bosses were as Capped as the rest of them, I decided.

But it hadn't all been for nothing. As I struggled to integrate with society, *The Tripods* provided some comfort. I watched the episodes over and over, and when the legend "Based on the Tripods trilogy by John Christopher" appeared in the opening titles, I would freeze the picture and yearn to meet the man who saw the world the way I did.

It was to be a good 20 years before I would. Jessica Kingsley Publishers were keen for me to secure an endorsement from the author. Well, I succeeded in making contact and he was only too happy to oblige. But he did more. He said that if ever I were in Rye in Sussex I would be welcome to pop in for a cup of tea and a chat. Naturally, I made sure I was in Rye in Sussex! And so, one November afternoon in 2004, I sat in the living room of Sam Youd (John Christopher), drinking tea and talking *Tripods*.

THE PRISONER

By my late teens, my closest friend and confidant was a pen pal I had never met. His name was Dominic, and I would regale him with my views on the world and society in general, sending recorded messages to him on audiotape. Then one morning, I received a package from him, a video of an old 1960s TV series that he thought I might identify with. And he was right!

A man, principled and angry, resigns from his high-profile government job. He thinks the reason for his resignation is none of his ex-employer's business. Once at home, nerve gas is pumped through the keyhole and he is rendered unconscious. When he wakes, he is no longer in London, but in a mysterious island community known only as The Village. It is a very colourful place and everyone seems really nice – disturbingly so. None of the residents have names, only numbers. The ever-changing Village chairman is Number Two, and the prisoner is Number Six. But who is Number One, the unseen governor of the prison?

The Prisoner is no ordinary spy series. It operates on many levels and explores the prison of society and the prison of one's own mind. The programme was the brainchild of its leading man, Patrick McGoohan, who, while filming in the scenic Welsh location of Portmeirion for an episode of *Danger Man*, saw its potential as a representation of the Global Village that the world had become thanks to advances in technology and communications. In this setting the Prisoner struggles to maintain his individualism while the system demands absolute conformity.

The various persons who take up the office of Number Two want any information he might be withholding, and Number Six determines that they won't get it. Throughout its 17 episodes, *The Prisoner* examines facets of society: the political system, the media and the press, the way we are educated, and the role of psychologists and psychiatrists, to name a few.

During my darkest days, I was completely obsessed with *The Prisoner*. Its message resonated deeply, as did the frustration of the central character. The series became the inspiration for my children's novel *The Blueprint*, an allegorical story where a teenage boy is dealt a blow to the head and then wakes to find himself in a nightmare parody of school life. You see, when I left school in 1986, I quickly realised (to my horror, I have to say) that secondary school is the blueprint for the world prison in which a few of us struggle to maintain our integrity.

Thanks to my wife Carol, the counselling I received on the NHS (National Health Service), and a diagnosis of Asperger syndrome, I have been able to turn the traumas of the past into dreams-come-true and publishing success. The four television programmes that helped me along the way now seem like old friends. To be honest, I still obsess about them, I think about them daily, but they are in their place.

At long last I have found where I belong in the real world.

Will amidst his sci-fi memorabilia

Will Hadcroft was born in 1970. He spent the whole of his teens wanting to fit in with various peer groups, but not on their terms. With no interest in competitive sports, an unorthodox taste in music, and crushing social phobia in select circumstances, he withdrew into the world of television science fiction. He married Carol in 1993, had sessions with a psychologist in 1995, and was diagnosed with Asperger syndrome in 2008.

Will is the author of the autobiographical account The Feeling's Unmutual *(published by Jessica Kingsley Publishers), the* Anne Droyd *series of adventures for children, and the young adult standalone novel* The Blueprint. *He now lives in Lancashire, UK.*